THE CRISIS OF PIETY

OTHER BOOKS BY DONALD G. BLOESCH

Centers of Christian Renewal
The Christian Life and Salvation
The Christian Witness in a Secular Age
Christian Spirituality East and West (coauthor)
The Reform of the Church
The Ground of Certainty
Servants of Christ (editor)
The Evangelical Renaissance
Wellsprings of Renewal
Light a Fire
The Invaded Church
Jesus is Victor! Karl Barth's Doctrine of Salvation
The Orthodox Evangelicals (coeditor)
Essentials of Evangelical Theology, Vol. I:
God, Authority and Salvation
Essentials of Evangelical Theology, Vol. II:
Life, Ministry and Hope
The Struggle of Prayer
Faith and its Counterfeits
Is the Bible Sexist?
The Future of Evangelical Christianity
Crumbling Foundations
The Battle for the Trinity
A Hermeneutics of Certitude (coauthor)
Freedom for Obedience

The CRISIS of PIETY

Essays toward a theology of the Christian life

Second Edition

Donald G. Bloesch

HELMERS & HOWARD

COLORADO SPRINGS

© 1988 by Donald G. Bloesch.

Published by Helmers & Howard, Publishers, Inc., P.O. Box 7407, Colorado Springs, CO 80933 USA.

Second edition (first publication in paperback). First edition published in 1968 by William B. Eerdmans Publishing Company.

Library of Congress Cataloging-in-Publication Data

Bloesch, Donald G., 1928-
    The crisis of piety : essays toward a theology of the
Christian life / Donald G. Bloesch. — 2nd ed.
      p.   cm.
    Includes bibliographical references and indexes.
    ISBN 0-939443-05-8
    1. Christian life—1960-   2. Spiritual life.   I. Title.
BV 4501.2.B56 1988
248—dc19   88-10989
                                                CIP

Printed in the United States of America

To
my mother,
Mrs. Adele Bloesch

ACKNOWLEDGMENTS

Several chapters in this book represent an expansion of earlier articles previously published in periodicals. Chapter Three, "The Crisis of Piety," first appeared in *The Covenant Quarterly*; Chapter Eight, "A Theology of Christian Commitment," was originally published in *Theology and Life*; Chapter Nine, "The Pilgrimage of Faith," previously appeared in *Encounter*; and the "Appendix on Liturgical Renewal" was first published in *Christianity Today*.

I wish to thank my wife, Brenda, for her careful reading of the manuscript and for her help in the indexing of this book.

CONTENTS

Author's Note   ix

Preface to First Edition   xv

1. Introduction: The Need for Spiritual Renewal   1

2. Theology at the Crossroads   7

3. The Crisis of Piety   25

4. The Mission of the Church: 37
   Spiritual or Secular?

5. Toward Recovery of the Devotional Life   49

6. The Meaning of Conversion   63

7. Two Types of Spirituality   81

8. A Theology of Christian Commitment   109

9. The Pilgrimage of Faith   121

   Appendix on Liturgical Renewal   143

   Index of Subjects   149

   Index of Names   153

   Index of Scripture   157

AUTHOR'S NOTE

WHEN DONALD SIMPSON proposed a new edition of my book *The Crisis of Piety* published by Eerdmans in 1968, I hesitated before accepting. I had to ask myself first of all if the issues of the sixties could still speak to people in our time. I also had to resolve the question of whether the need for cultivating the Christian life should remain the focus of theology.

In some respects the situation in the sixties and our situation are remarkably similar. To be sure, the main emphasis in that earlier period was the overthrow of oppressive social structures, whereas spirituality plays a prominent role today. The concern for deepening the inner life was nonetheless present in the sixties, as was evidenced in the Jesus movement and the fascination with Eastern mysticism. Moreover, the spirituality currently in fashion is increasingly being tied to movements of social liberation. There is admittedly a more materialistic bent among our young people, but the emergence of the electronic church and the proliferation of the cults attest the spiritual hunger that is pervasive in our society.

The heresies of the sixties are not quite the same as those of today. In that period we were confronted with the death of God theology, secular theology, and the theology of revolution. While the first proved to be shortlived, we now see theological movements that stand in direct continuity with the old: liberation theology, feminist theology, and black theology, all of which are pressing for a new social order characterized by justice and freedom. We are also witnessing a refurbished process theology and the rebirth of neo-mystical theology, which was very much alive in the sixties.

Today people are much more conscious of the influence of ideology in shaping our moral and spiritual decisions. Ideology is here understood as the often unconscious alignment with forces in society that serve to insure our economic security or advance our cultural status. Ideology was certainly rampant in the sixties, but we are becoming much more aware of the ideological factor in the social stances of the churches.

One startling change in the religious situation is the erosion of ecumenism and the rise of a militant brand of evangelical and fundamentalist religion. The ecumenical movement still continues, but most Christians are presently more concerned with church growth and expansion than with church unity. Yet it will become increasingly clear that there can be no solid Christian advance until the age-old barriers that divide the churches begin crumbling, for nothing so disillusions the peoples of the Third World as divisiveness in the ranks of the people of God.

Church unity will not come, however, apart from grappling with the issues of faith and order that comprise the basis for Christian mission. The popularity of secular ecumenism — unity on the basis of social commitment — has served to push faith and order concerns into the background. But a consensus on social issues will ultimately disintegrate unless it is grounded in a common vision and a common dogma. We already see this on the issues of abortion, prayer in the public schools, homosexuality, and population control.

One cannot but welcome the new interest in spirituality in academic religious circles, but upon closer examination much of the spirituality in question proves to be based on the cultural quest for meaning rather than loyalty to the biblical imperatives. The spiritual formation that is at the fore bears an uncanny resemblance to the group dynamics in vogue in the sixties and early seventies. The kind of spirituality generally advocated today is a far cry from what I have called *piety*, fear and trust in the living God.

Secularism is still alive and well, even when it takes the form of religiosity. A candid examination of the official pronouncements of the churches more often than not reveals an ideological captivity rather than a prophetic perceptivity.

The question remains: Can the new wine of the gospel be poured into the old wineskins of the institutional churches? It may be that the hope of the church lies in the movement of the Spirit raising up new forms of Christian witness and service that do not negate the wider church but serve to reform and purify it. I am thinking among other things of new kinds of Bible colleges where the focus would be on the renewal of the churches as well as on mission to the world. The Bible colleges of evangelicalism have generally called people out of the established churches into missionary service that competes with rather than supplements the endeavors of the churches. These new forms of Christian witness would be analogous to the Catholic monasteries of the middle ages, functioning as lighthouses to the churches as well as to a lost and dying world. An important difference is that these pioneering ventures would be solidly grounded in the gospel of free grace and committed to the primacy and divine authority of Holy Scripture. Like the monastic orders, they would make an earnest effort to be accountable in some way to the larger church.

I believe that my book remains relevant because the relation of social concern and personal piety has not been resolved. Evangelicals are involved in the same kinds of compromises that they accused liberals of a generation ago: bringing the gospel into the service of a particular political agenda. The search for signs and evidences for faith continues unabated, striking a responsive chord in the fragile human heart. The inordinate attention given to the Shroud of Turin is a recent example of the audacious but ill-fated attempt to gain evidential certainty for faith. Mysticism proves to be a perennial temptation for Christians, though the emphasis for some time has been on making contact with the creativity in nature rather than on flight to a world beyond.

If there has been a shift in my perspective, I believe more strongly than before that a theology of Christian commitment must be united with a theology of the Word of God if it is not to lapse into subjectivism and anthropocentrism. The focus on personal piety must never supplant the more basic focus on the life, death, and resurrection of Jesus Christ. The bane of classical Pietism was that it sought to cultivate the Christian life without a corresponding

xiiTHE CRISIS OF PIETY

emphasis on the decision of God for humanity in Jesus Christ. Morality and Christian character became more important than the incarnation and substitutionary atonement of Christ in biblical history. Pietism invariably fades into latitudinarianism and liberalism unless it is informed by the wisdom of orthodoxy. Orthodoxy, on the other hand, becomes barren and deadening unless it is nurtured by an abiding seriousness concerning personal salvation and the life of discipleship. What is called for is a live orthodoxy, which is none other than a biblically grounded and theologically robust Pietism.

I have added an "Appendix on Liturgical Renewal," not included in the original edition. This was written in roughly the same period as the other essays in this book. Because there is presently a movement among evangelicals toward a more high church form of worship, I thought it well to include this material. It also has relevance in the light of the creeping sacramentalism and liturgism in the mainline churches. The crisis in personal piety is indubitably related to the crisis in corporate worship. James White, Robert Webber, and others rightly criticize the poverty in the worship services of popular evangelicalism where people come to be entertained rather than to praise the living God. Yet it is questionable whether the retreat to high-churchism can be the answer to the crisis of piety.

Evangelicals need to rediscover the sacraments but at the same time be wary of sacramentalism. We need to recover the beauty of holiness without falling into the aesthetic temptation of finding holiness in beauty. We need to rediscover the church as a sacramental community without losing sight of the importance of a regenerate church membership.

The crisis of piety is also manifested in the crisis in personal morality, and this is more evident in mainline churches and theological schools than it was two decades ago. The startling rise in divorce among the clergy, the glaring incapacity of churches to discipline their wayward members, and the concerted attempts within the churches to ordain professed homosexuals are all signs of moral disarray in a supposedly Christian society. Yet the answer to this crisis lies not in a return to the legalism of taboos but in a rebirth of confidence in the healing and regenerating power of the one Lord

— Jesus Christ — as he speaks to us in the Bible and in the fathers and mothers of the church through the ages.

In a time when many gospels are competing with one gospel, we should seek a renewed commitment to the truth of the gospel proclaimed by the apostles and the Reformers as well as a telling demonstration of this truth in our daily lives. Faith and life go together, but being precedes doing. And this means that inward communion with the living Christ made possible by the outpouring of the Holy Spirit is the basis for both church reform and social holiness.

1988

PREFACE TO FIRST EDITION

THESE ESSAYS WERE written over a period of several years and reflect a definite progression in my thought concerning the need for a new kind of theology for our day. The introduction was written last in order to summarize the principal themes under discussion.

In my theological development there has been a growing concern for a renewal of personal devotion to Jesus Christ. Such a concern is shared by many others today including John Mackay, Adolf Köberle, Bernard Häring, Emile Cailliet, Elton Trueblood, Mother Basilea Schlink, and Jack Winslow. The church has not been silent in the face of social evils, and yet its word seems to lack power and discriminating judgment. The churches are immersed not so much in the real issues of our time, whether they be doctrinal or moral, as in peripheral concerns, most of which pertain to the maintaining of their organizational machinery. Little if any consideration is given to the life of devotion and prayer. Sunday School curricula for the most part seek to acquaint people with the biblical and ecclesiastical traditions of the church, but the themes of justification, prayer, piety, and conversion are practically ignored. Some of the radical theologians are rightly calling the attention of the church to social ills and injustices that need to be corrected. Yet can there be genuine social reformation apart from personal transformation?

The name of Dietrich Bonhoeffer is being eulogized today by many who misunderstand the real thrust of his message. Bonhoeffer sought the penetration of the world by the gospel, but he maintained that such penetration could not occur apart from an arcane discipline of devotion. It was his intention to bring the spiritual to bear upon the secular, but he never equated the two. This is not to imply that Bonhoeffer himself is beyond criticism. What he lacked was a theology of the demonic, which would have called into question certain ideas that he developed, such as "the man come of age." Yet it cannot be denied that he stands within the mainstream of the evangelical tradition, and if he were living today he would surely refuse to be identified with the theology of some of his followers.

If Bonhoeffer failed to take seriously the reality of the demonic, this can be said even more of the secular or radical theologians, such as J. A. T. Robinson, James Pike, William Hamilton, Howard Moody, Thomas Altizer, and Harvey Cox. These men view the world through the rose-colored glasses of modernity and thereby end in practically identifying the sacred and the profane. For some of these people Christian secularity means the acceptance of profanity, obscenity, and premarital and extramarital sex. In the light of the articles by Cox and Hamilton in *Playboy* magazine and the contributions of Cox, Pike, and Moody to the symposium on religion and the new morality in the same magazine (June, 1967), it would appear that these men have embraced at least some of the tenets of that particular brand of hedonism. Altizer and Hamilton seem to have capitulated to the new hedonism by viewing sex as the emerging realm of the sacred.

Certainly we must recover the biblical truth that the world as created is good and that it was ordained to be the theater of God's glory. Yet we must also take into consideration the stark reality of sin and the subjugation of the world by what Paul calls the powers of darkness. George MacLeod is more biblical and realistic than the secular theologians when he states in an article in the Iona Community magazine *The Coracle* (Dec. 16, 1966): "By all means say that the secular is the realm of God's activity and that He is in and through all things. But realize He has both let loose Satan there, for our disciplining, and that Christ is also there for our salvation."

In my view Christians should not be children of the times but rather prophets to the times. What is needed is something more drastic than creative disaffiliation from the trivialities of the culture as advocated by Harvey Cox. Rather the church should be in active opposition to the idolatrous spirit and false values of our secularized culture. The church should not accommodate itself to but rather seek to unmask the cultural gods of militarism, nationalism, and hedonism.

We need once more to recognize that the principal conflict today as in every day is not that between Communism and capitalism or that between science and religion. It is not even that between the sacred and the secular, since both are authorized and sanctioned by God. Rather the conflict is between faith and unbelief, light and darkness, salvation and sin. When we recover this essential truth of the gospel, we shall then be able to march forth into the culture and wrestle with and overcome the principalities and powers.

The church needs to rediscover its spiritual mission, which is to uphold the biblical message of salvation before the world. Yet this does not abrogate its responsibility to speak to the crucial issues of our time. Indeed, if the church is truly focused upon the command- ments and promises of God revealed in the Bible, it will be moved to bring this revelation to bear upon the whole society, including the political and economic life of man. For the Christian is called to obedience not simply in the private sphere of life but in the public sphere as well. Yet the Christian will always be a stranger and exile in this world. His motivations and goals will be radically different from those of the man of the world, since he belongs to a spiritual Lord and his citizenship is in heaven.

We have placed too much hope in politics and social reforms, only to find out that we were being deprived of our most precious possession: our spiritual life. It is trampled by the party mob in the East, by the commercial one in the West. We are at a harsh spiritual crisis and a political impasse. All the celebrated technological achievements of progress . . . do not redeem the 20th century's moral poverty.

Alexander Solzhenitsyn

The issue can no longer be evaded. It is becoming clearer every day that the most urgent problem besetting our Church is this: How can we live the Christian life in the modern world?

Dietrich Bonhoeffer

One

INTRODUCTION: THE NEED FOR SPIRITUAL RENEWAL

THE EROSION OF FAITH

OUR AGE CURRENTLY finds itself in a crisis of faith. Too many people have only a speculative and not an experiential knowledge of the truth of faith. The reality of God has become hypothetical even for many who call themselves Christians. Such terms as "the silence of God," "the eclipse of God," "the absence of God," and "the death of God" are now very much in vogue. One symptom of the breakdown in faith is the loss of piety, meaning by that the fear of God. Spiritual disciplines such as prayer and fasting are foreign to most modern Christians. The hymn that begins with the words, "Take time to be holy, Speak oft with thy Lord," has little meaning in our secularized church and culture. In an age of the death of God prayer has become problematical even for those who are active in the church. In the words of R. Gregor Smith: "It is probably not an exaggeration to say that the vast mass of even conscientious church members have entirely relinquished the habit of private prayer in any of the conventional forms."[1]

Hand in hand with the dissipation of faith is a crisis in communication. Secular theologians contend that the language of the faith is no longer meaningful to modern man. According to Bultmann, the archaic picture-language of the Bible needs to be demythologized if

---

[1] R. Gregor Smith, *Secular Christianity* (London: Collins, 1966), p. 207.

1

it is to be made comprehensible to the secular culture. Harvey Cox suggests that we utilize political instead of religious language to communicate the central truth of the faith to the unbelieving world. William Hordern, on the other hand, maintains that God-talk is still necessary particularly for Christian theology, and he bases his case partly on insights drawn from the school of analytic philosophy.[2]

What we are witnessing today is the advent of secularization, a turning of man's attention from the other world to this world. This in itself is not a disaster, since we are called to work out our spiritual vocation in the midst of the grime and agony of this world. Yet when people become preoccupied with the things of this world, when they become immersed in penultimate rather than ultimate concerns, the spiritual dimension of life becomes empty. The secularization of the churches can be seen in the attention that they give to finance and organization rather than to the study of Scripture and prayer. Such churches can no longer speak the Word of God with power, since they are no longer sure what they believe. They have for all practical purposes succumbed to the ideology of the culture.

Some theologians hail the process of secularization as an emancipation from the superstitions and outmoded beliefs of an earlier period in history. They speak after the manner of Bonhoeffer of a "world come of age" and of "man come of age." There is truth in the view that the secularization of modern culture may be a mixed blessing, and yet can we also discern the perils in a culture where the very reality of God is called into question? It can be said that when God is dead, then man is dead, since man derives the meaning of his existence from the One who is his Creator. One might also affirm that the death of God prepares the way for the reappearance of the gods, the idols that seek to fill the metaphysical and spiritual vacuum of the culture.

Perhaps we can agree that man has reached a certain level of intellectual maturity and sophistication. Indeed, he has at his disposal a wealth of knowledge that was simply inaccessible in past eras. But has he thereby attained moral and spiritual maturity? His technical superiority over his forefathers is unquestioned, but does he have wisdom? If the ultimate goal is technical knowledge and power, then modern man can be said to have come of age. But if the

---

[2] See William Hordern, *Speaking of God* (New York: Macmillan, 1964).

goal is the meaning of ultimate existence, then man has descended to a new infancy (Abraham Heschel).

What is needed today is a renewal of devotion to the living Savior, Jesus Christ. Such renewal will take the form of a spiritual reformation that involves the very structure and life of the church. It will take the form of a deepening concern for prayer and meditation. It will also manifest itself in an awakened interest in the sacraments, particularly the Blessed Sacrament of Holy Communion. Surely a renewed devotion to Jesus Christ will also entail a passionate concern for the outcasts and unfortunates in our world, those who have been made homeless by war and famine, the victims of racial apartheid, and the diseased and forsaken.

Yet it is to be recognized that authentic renewal finally rests upon a new outpouring of the Holy Spirit. Indeed, it is only the Spirit that enables us to pray and to preach with power and conviction. It is the Spirit who empowers us for service in the kingdom of God. It is the Spirit who pours meaning into the language of faith and who enlightens those to whom this language is addressed. The renewal of devotion in our time will entail a rediscovery of the role of the Holy Spirit in Christian faith and practice.

DEVOTION AND DOCTRINE

One cannot speak of the renewal of devotion without stressing the importance of theology. Devotion to Jesus Christ cannot long maintain itself apart from theological fidelity and integrity. [A holy life divorced from sound doctrine soon becomes moralism. At the same time correct doctrine apart from a holy life is nothing other than intellectualism.] In the circles of popular "pietism," for example, Moral Re-Armament and Camps Farthest Out, one often detects a disparagement of theology. We are told that what matters is not so much what one believes as how one lives. This kind of orientation reflects the dictum of Schleiermacher: "It matters not what conceptions a man adheres to, he can still be pious."[3] Such thinking has penetrated deeply into Protestant liberal theology.

---

[3] Friedrich Schleiermacher, *On Religion* (trans. John Oman), (New York: Harper & Row, 1958), p. 95.

At the same time we must also beware of disparaging piety. Indeed, one cannot really know the truth unless one is devoted to the truth (Pascal). Doctrine is lifeless apart from inward commitment. The separation of faith from commitment was precisely one of the errors against which the Protestant Reformers protested Luther and Calvin both contended that faith consists not simply in intellectual assent to dogma but in heartfelt trust and confidence in a living Savior *(fiducia cordis)*. It is only this kind of faith that makes the salvation of Christ effectual in people's lives. We therefore conclude that doctrinal theology *(theologia dogmatica)* should be held in balance with a theology of spiritual life or devotion *(theologia vitae spiritualis)*.

We need also today to perceive the integral relationship between the life of devotion and Christian salvation. Is consecrated devotion only a sign and mirror of a salvation procured for us in the past? Or is it not the means by which this salvation is realized and made concrete in our lives? I hold to the latter position. I affirm that the life of devotion is the battleground on which our salvation is fought for and continually recovered. It is not the cause of our justification, but it is a major factor in the implementation of justification in the world. It is a means by which the fruits of Christ's past sacrifice are appropriated in the present. Not on account of our works, and yet not apart from our works — this indeed is the position of both Calvin and Jonathan Edwards.

HALLMARKS OF BIBLICAL PIETY

In seeking to formulate a theology of Christian life, we must take care to differentiate biblical piety from all kinds of pseudo-piety Biblical piety is first of all characterized by inward devotion to the Savior, Jesus Christ. It entails daily repentance under the cross of Christ and renewed dedication to the will of Christ. Such dedication will be manifested in every area of life, including the public or political sphere of life. True piety also involves a sharpening of our critical faculties, since the closer we grow toward God the more aware we become of the need for discriminating between truth and error. Our love should abound with both knowledge and discernment (Phil. 1:9); this means that we should test everything in the light of the Word of God. That kind of religion which is open to every whim or fancy has no moorings, whereas Christian devotion is anchored in the biblical revelation, the faith once delivered to the saints (Jude 3).

Friedrich Schleiermacher spoke much about the recovery of piety, and yet it is important to distinguish my position from his. For Schleiermacher piety consists essentially in a feeling of absolute dependence upon God. The accent in his theology was upon resignation and surrender. I view piety much more in terms of obedience — not only spiritual but also ethical obedience. Moreover, I understand theology not as an account of religious affections set forth in speech but rather as a systematic explication of biblical revelation. Religious experience cannot be the source or norm of theology, but it is the channel through which the message of faith is mediated.

I also take issue with Schleiermacher when he affirms that there are other "bibles" comparable to Scripture that serve to awaken piety.[4] I hold that no one can attain true piety unless he has first been confronted with the biblical message of the cross, of how Christ suffered and died for our sins. This means that Holy Scripture, being the veritable vessel of the gospel, is the principal source of all piety. This is not to deny that other devotional writings may be used in our spiritual life as a supplement to Scripture, but they should be fully in accord with the biblical proclamation. The pious person will derive spiritual aid from various sources but will look to the Bible above all for illumination and consolation.

Karl Barth has been very reluctant to expatiate upon piety, undoubtedly in reaction to the distortion of true piety in the Schleiermacherian theology of religious experience. Yet it is a mistake to suppose that Barth is opposed to a pious life; on the contrary, he affirms the need for true piety. He has written concerning biblical piety:

> Biblical *piety* is conscious of its own limits, of its relativity. In its essence it is humility, fear of the Lord. It points beyond the world, and points at the same time and above all beyond itself. It lives absolutely by virtue of its Object and for its Object.[5]

---

[4] *Ibid.*, pp. 249, 250.

[5] Karl Barth, *The Word of God and the Word of Man* (trans. Douglas Horton), (New York: Harper & Row, 1957), p. 69.

Barth's conception is sound up to a point. Yet we must ask whether piety has to do exclusively with the Giver of faith and not at all with the subject of faith. Our chief obligation should be to give glory to God, but should we not also be concerned for the salvation of man? We are told to fear God and to give him glory (Rev. 14:7). But we are also urged to work out our salvation in fear and trembling (Phil. 2:12).

Biblical piety will be centered upon the cross of Christ, for it is there that our salvation was procured. But such piety will also concern itself with the bearing of the cross by believers. It will be at the same time fully theocentric and radically anthropocentric, since it is related to both the glory of God and the restoration and well-being of humanity.

When Christians again place their fear and trust in the living God; when they seek to draw close to the spiritual wellsprings of faith in prayer and devotion; when they seek to imitate their Savior in a life of outgoing loving service to others, then the secular age will pay heed to their gospel, and perhaps once more God will become meaningful to people. An age that has experienced the death of God needs now to experience the power of the resurrection of his Son in the lives of believers. And the remnant of the faithful need to be filled and empowered by the Spirit of God so that they can give an intelligible and compelling witness to a world groping in the darkness of sin and plagued by the anxiety of meaninglessness.

Two

THEOLOGY
AT THE CROSSROADS

THE SEARCH FOR A NEW THEOLOGY

THE CONTEMPORARY CHURCH is in a state of theological fer-
ment. Traditional theological positions are now under fire
from various quarters. The old theological clichés and categories
are being critically reexamined, and for the most part they are found
to be wanting. The age-old battle between Protestantism and
Catholicism carries little weight on the modern theological scene.
The warfare between liberalism and fundamentalism is also outdated, although some of the issues remain unresolved.

Many of those who have been nurtured on neo-orthodoxy are
finding that the emphases of that particular school of theology are
no longer relevant or adequate. They are pointing to certain defi-
ciencies in that theology which need to be remedied. Whereas the
neo-orthodox theologians placed the accent upon Christ for us, the
younger generation of students is asking whether Scripture does not
give equal weight to Christ with us and Christ in us. They are also
seeking to give more attention to the sacraments, which have been
sorely neglected by nearly all the leading figures of neo-orthodoxy.
Again there is a desire on the part of a new generation to take the
reality of the demonic much more seriously than did the older
theologians. The genocide of six million Jews by the Nazis and the
increasing barbarism of modern warfare (as reflected in the use of
biological and nuclear weapons) have awakened people to the stark

7

reality of the demonic. Emil Brunner was among those who did affirm the existence of a supernatural power of evil, but he did not develop this idea, and it has little significance in his system. To the credit of the neo-orthodox theologians they called the church back to its divine standard and source, viz., the revelation of God in Jesus Christ attested in Holy Scripture, and those who seek to construct a new theology today can certainly build on no other foundation.

The erstwhile sons of Protestant fundamentalism are likewise seeking to move beyond the older theology into something new. William Hordern speaks of "the new face of conservatism," by which he means the attempt on the part of conservatives to give a fresh and compelling restatement of the Christian witness.[1] Carl Henry has written a book entitled *The Uneasy Conscience of Modern Fundamentalism* (1947), in which he deplores the reluctance of fundamentalists to speak out on moral issues (such as the race problem). Billy Graham has annoyed many conservatives by calling for a Protestant appreciation of Mary. He has also aroused misgivings among some right-wing biblicists by maintaining that the belief in the deity of Christ rather than the verbal inspiration of the Bible should be the basis for Christian fellowship. Conservative theologians such as George Eldon Ladd and A. Berkeley Mickelsen have even gone so far as to accept the historical criticism of Scripture, although they dissociate themselves from destructive rationalistic criticism.[2]

There is a desire on the part of those who belong to the historic churches of the Protestant Reformation to move beyond confessionalism. It was Bonhoeffer who contended that the old themes of confessional orthodoxy, such as the atonement, regeneration, etc., are no longer meaningful to many people.[3] This, of course, must not be taken to mean that we will be able to reach the secular man by abandoning these doctrines. But it does imply that something more than doctrinal loyalty is needed if the secular world is to be won for the gospel. Christoph Blumhardt, one of the last great figures of Pietism, was already very critical of a rigid confessional stance:

[1] See William Hordern, *New Directions in Theology Today: Introduction* (Philadelphia: Westminster, 1966), pp. 74-95.
[2] See George E. Ladd, *The New Testament and Criticism* (Grand Rapids: Eerdmans, 1967) and A. Berkeley Mickelsen, *Interpreting the Bible* (Grand Rapids: Eerdmans, 1963).
[3] Dietrich Bonhoeffer, *Letters and Papers from Prison* (trans. Reginald Fuller), (New York: Macmillan, 1953), p. 187.

"Now it is no longer a matter of confessions and churches; those times are over. Certainly I do not want to be one who overthrows things, but in actual fact what is left is nothing but ruins."[4] And in the words of his father, Johann Christoph Blumhardt: "To insist on symbols [creedal statements], not wanting to go further than they lead, is very dangerous."[5]

Theologians today are speaking of the need for spirituality. They are insisting that a theology of proclamation has to be supplemented by a theology of devotion. They are pointing to the need for a reformation of life as well as of doctrine. Bonhoeffer reflected this new mood in his criticism of the Confessing Church in Germany: "The over-all achievement of the Confessing Church: championing ecclesiastical interests, but little personal faith in Jesus Christ."[6]

The so-called Lundensian school of theology in Sweden (Nygren, Aulén) has sought to define theology as a strictly scientific and historical discipline. But a rising complaint against this school is that it abstracts theology from life.[7] In contrast to the Lundensians Kierkegaard spoke of truth as "inwardness" and "passion." He also said: "The highest of all is not to understand the highest but to act upon it." The Kierkegaardian posture continues to be appreciated by the younger generation of theologians, whereas the neo-orthodox and neo-Lutheran theologies are being increasingly subjected to criticism.

Theological students today are also yearning for a deeper sacramental life within Protestantism. Paul Tillich found a ready response from many students when he contended that the Protestant principle must be united with Catholic substance (by which he meant the sacraments) if it is to survive. In the ecumenical age in which we live the sacraments are once again a live issue as Protestants are moving towards a new appreciation of the Catholic tradition. The liturgical movement has abetted the new interest in the sacraments on the part of both Catholics and Protestants.

Finally, there is the desire of many younger theologians for social relevance. Bonhoeffer again has played a major role in seeking to

---

[4] R. Lejeune, ed., *Christoph Blumhardt and His Message* (Rifton, N.Y.: Plough, 1963), p. 54.

[5] *Ibid.*, p. 28.

[6] Bonhoeffer, *Letters and Papers from Prison*, p. 237.

[7] See Deane William Ferm, "Sex, Sin and Salvation in Sweden," in *The Christian Century*, LXXXIII, no. 38 (Sept. 21, 1966), pp. 1142-1146.

relate the ultimate concerns of the faith to the penultimate concerns of life in this world. He pointed out in his *Letters and Papers from Prison* that the life of the Christian today must be one that is under God but also one that is lived out in this world. The other-worldly orientation of faith must be balanced by a this-worldly concern. This is why Bonhoeffer spoke of God as "the beyond in the midst" as over against the deistic other-worldly God of traditional piety. Reinhold Niebuhr, of course, stated the case for social relevance even before Bonhoeffer. And prior to Niebuhr there was the Social Gospel movement represented by such men as Walter Rauschenbusch. Yet never before has there been such a deep concern on the part of Christians everywhere for service to the outcasts and unfortunates in the world.

New Theological Alternatives

In this section I propose to examine some of the theological alternatives that are being considered by the church today. It is my view that all of these positions are lacking in some fundamental area, although this is not to deny that each has something to offer.

First we should consider neo-liberalism, which essentially represents an attempt by theologians to utilize philosophy in order to communicate to the secular age. Whereas the older liberalism was characterized by a belief in the moral progress of man, the new liberalism takes into consideration the estrangement of man and the power of evil in the world. Both types of liberalism are apologetic, in that they seek to make the faith palatable or acceptable to modern man. There are various schools of theology within the category of neo-liberalism including Tillich's ecstatic naturalism, the neo-naturalism of Ogden, Cobb, and Wieman, which leans heavily upon process philosophy, and the existentialist theologies of Bultmann and Ebeling. To the credit of all these men they are calling the attention of the intellectuals to the claims of the faith. Where they go astray is in failing to recognize that it is only the Spirit of God working through the message of the cross that can bring people into the kingdom. Apologetic argument may gain a hearing for the faith, but it often makes the natural man more defensive and intransigent in his position.

Another living option in Protestant theology today is secular or radical theology. This current of thought has also been called religionless Christianity and renewal activism. One can here list such thinkers as Harvey Cox, J. A. T. Robinson, William Hamilton, and R. Gregor Smith. The death-of-God theology is one strand within the larger school of secular theology. The emphasis in this type of theology is not on a correlation with philosophy but rather on service to the outcasts and needy in the world. It is not dialogue with the creative disciplines of the culture (although this is also present) but rather *diakonia* that is regarded as the principal means of reaching the secular man of today. Whereas the neo-liberals seek to correlate the Christian religion and secular philosophy, the radicals seek to move beyond religion into a secular faith. In this type of theology we find a marked optimism concerning human capabilities compared to the pessimism of neo-orthodoxy. Whereas Barth and Brunner stressed human helplessness and misery, the secular theologians sound the call to heroism. Secular theology can be appreciated for calling our attention to the truth that our belief should make a difference in our economic and social attitudes. Yet in its attempt to make the faith relevant to a secular culture this theology has been led to obscure if not deny the transcendence of God (and in some instances the very reality of God), as well as the free grace of Christ, which alone can be the basis for Christian optimism. It is also highly questionable whether the concept of heroism espoused by radical theologians is equivalent to sainthood as this has been understood in the church through the ages. It is interesting to note that these theologians speak of the need for secular saints.[8]

Still another theological option today is ecumenical theology. Here we might consider such names as Robert McAfee Brown, Eugene Carson Blake, Douglas Horton, Albert Outler, and Gregory Baum. Insofar as this type of theology seeks to muster and combine the resources of the various Christian bodies for the salvation of the world, it can be regarded as a sign of renewal in the church today. One danger is that church union might come to be viewed as an end in itself, without any concern for the conversion of the lost. Another is that Christian unity may be based on the least common denominator rather than on the total biblical and catholic witness to Jesus Christ. It is probably right that Jews be included in ecumenical

---

[8] For an excellent critique of modern radical theology from an evangelical, biblical viewpoint see Kenneth Hamilton, *Revolt Against Heaven* (Grand Rapids: Eerdmans, 1965) and his *God is Dead: The Anatomy of a Slogan* (Eerdmans, 1966).

conversations, but some theologians argue that missions to the Jews are no longer tenable. This is an ecumenical eclecticism that is certainly at variance with gospel Christianity.

Within the ecumenical movement there has emerged a strand of thought that is sometimes called "secular ecumenism" because it seeks unity on the basis of the performance of common tasks in the world.[9] Here one can discern the convergence of the new secular theology and ecumenical theology. The Ecumenical Institute in Chicago certainly mirrors a secular ecumenism. The whole emphasis at the Institute is not on changing man's nature but on improving man's lot. But Christianity then becomes only another form of humanitarianism. Jesus Christ is then no longer the Savior of the lost but only a shining example of sacrificial love.

I support the movement for Christian unity, since I believe that it is Christ's will that his church be one, but at the same time I hold that this movement stands in need of deeper theological grounding. True unity can finally be achieved not on the basis of love or good will alone but rather on the basis of truth. Such ecumenists as John Mackay and Bela Vassady point to the need for being evangelical as well as ecumenical if the church is to live in obedience to the gospel of Jesus Christ.

Mention should also be made in this connection of the theological movement which sometimes goes under the name of evangelical Catholicism. This is in a sense one of the fruits of the ecumenical movement. It is to be distinguished from eclectic ecumenical theology in that it seeks a solid theological basis for church union, one that is grounded in the biblical message of free grace propounded by the Evangelical Reformation and also one that is anchored in the interpretation of this message in the catholic tradition. Some of those who are active in this movement, such as Max Lackmann, President of the League for Evangelical-Catholic Reunion, seek a corporate reunion of Protestantism with the Roman church. Lackmann envisages a church united under the papacy of Rome but characterized by liturgical diversity and a great amount of freedom concerning the divisive doctrines of the past. My objection to this kind of Evangelical Catholicism is that it seeks for unity before doctrinal consensus, which is a serious error. Such a

---

9 See George Lindbeck, "Secular Ecumenism in Action" and Albert Van Den Heuvel, "Secular Ecumenism and the Teaching of the Faith," *The Catholic World*, CCV, no. 1225 (April, 1967), pp. 7-19.

theology should probably better be called Evangelical Romanism than Evangelical Catholicism.

This is not to deny, however, that Lackmann's movement offers many positive contributions, to which ecumenically-minded Christians would do well to give serious attention. Also to be included in the general school of Evangelical Catholicism are Jaroslav Pelikan, Hans Asmussen, Max Thurian, and J. L. Leuba. One of the dangers in this movement is that it focuses its attention upon the glorious catholic heritage of the past rather than a new kind of church in the future. It seeks to overcome the crisis of piety by a reappropriation of the sacramental riches of the catholic tradition, but does not the key to renewal today lie in repentance for personal and national sins and also for the sins of the church? These theologians rightly remind us that the Bible must always be read and interpreted *within* the church, but they sometimes tend to forget that the church must always stand *under* the Bible insofar as the biblical message is the sole and infallible criterion for church dogma and doctrine. Some of these people seek not a return to Rome but a breakthrough into a new form of the church, yet one that is in direct continuity with the catholic tradition. This movement has much promise, and perhaps it contains the key to church renewal.

Finally consideration should be given to the new conservatism or neo-evangelicalism, the movement that seeks to replace fundamentalism as a viable option for modern Christians. That this school contains much that is creative and original is suggested by the fact that it is under constant attack by the more authentic fundamentalists such as Robert Lightner, the two Bob Joneses, Cornelius Van Til, and Carl McIntire.[10] The bane of this new movement is biblicism, which might be defined as viewing the Bible as an authority in and of itself. The dogmatic norm of the Protestant Reformers was not the Bible as such but rather the Word of God given in the Bible by the Spirit. There is also a tendency in the new conservative movement to perpetuate the fundamentalist doctrine of biblical inerrancy. The Bible is, of course, inerrant regarding the truth that it proclaims, but because of the ambiguities of this word I believe that it is better to speak of the Bible as fully reliable or

---

[10] For a scholarly critique of the new conservatives from the standpoint of Protestant fundamentalism see Robert Lightner, *Neo-Evangelicalism*, 2nd ed. (Des Plaines, Ill.: Regular Baptist Press, 1965).

trustworthy.[11] Some of the new conservatives hold that the Bible is the only infallible rule for faith and practice but that it is not a perfect measuring rod on matters of history and science; this position, however, is hotly contested.[12] Many of those who embrace a conservative theology acknowledge that errors have crept into the Bible through copying and translating, but they hold to the inerrancy of the autographs (which are no longer extant). The evangelical scholar Jack Rogers maintains that the idea of inerrant autographs actually represents a deviation from the theology of the Westminster divines.[13] We need once again to recover the paradox that the Bible is both the infallible Word of God and the words of finite and sinful men who were, however, guided by the Spirit of God. We need to understand the Bible not as a document that can be proved or disproved, but as a sacrament, a veritable means of grace.

To their credit many of the new conservatives are now defining revelation in dynamic rather than static terms.[14] Some of them are also holding that there is an inseparable connection between revelation and the Bible, but not an absolute identity. A significant few are perceiving that the Word of God cannot be frozen in the pages of Scripture, just as it cannot be packaged by the clerics of the church.

---

[11] I also consider the term infallibility more acceptable than inerrancy when applied to Scripture. The connotations of the former are religious and confessional whereas those of the latter are scientific and apologetic.

[12] For a conservative criticism of the concept of biblical inerrancy see Dewey Beegle, *The Inspiration of Scripture* (Philadelphia: Westminster, 1963). Beegle has done a good piece of work, but there still remains the need for a statement on biblical inspiration that does justice to the divine authority as well as the cultural limitations of the Bible. The whole question of biblical inspiration and authority was reappraised at a conference of conservative evangelical scholars held at Gordon College and Divinity School (Wenham, Mass.) in June, 1966. For a report on this conference see *Christianity Today*, X, no. 21 (July 22, 1966), pp. 27, 41.

[13] See Jack B. Rogers, *Scripture in the Westminster Confession* (Grand Rapids: Eerdmans, 1967). This excellent scholarly work, which is a doctoral thesis written under G. C. Berkouwer, should be read by all who seek a new statement on biblical inspiration.

[14] Robert Boyd has written: "In one sense the whole problem of . . . communicating the Christian faith, lies in the fact . . . that the God in whom the Christian believes is not the Object of propositions that one can set about proving or disproving, but the Subject of encounter, an encounter centered on our moral response to Christ" (in D. M. MacKay, ed., *Christianity In a Mechanistic Universe* (Chicago: Inter-Varsity, 1965), p. 122. And from Kenneth Kantzer: ". . . the ultimate goal of revelation is not so much to make man wise as it is to bring him into a direct encounter with God as a person, and to evoke from him a response of love and obedience to God" ("The Authority of the Bible," in M. C. Tenney, ed., *The Word for This Century* [New York: Oxford, 1960], p. 34).

The movement as a whole reminds us that the truth of revelation does contain some propositional elements as well. It also compels us to rethink the doctrine of biblical inspiration. Neo-orthodoxy has said much about revelation but very little about inspiration, and consequently it has been unable to do justice to the divine ground of Scripture.

My main difficulty with the new conservatives (and I speak as one who is doctrinally conservative) is that they do not fully perceive that the real issue today is not the authenticity and inerrancy of the text of Scripture but rather the Christian life in a secular culture. The third-force Protestants (the Holiness and Pentecostal churches) see this better than the mainstream of evangelical conservatism. Peace churches, such as the Mennonites and the Church of the Brethren, also recognize that the paramount concern today should be Christian obedience. Bonhoeffer has stated my position well: "It is becoming clearer every day that the most urgent problem besetting our Church is this: How can we live the Christian life in the modern world?"[15] There is a new interest in social sanctification on the part of the neo-evangelicals, and the theological vitality of this movement may yet prepare the way for genuine Christian renewal in our time.[16]

EVANGELICAL DEVOTIONISM

As a fresh alternative for the church today I propose a theology of evangelical devotion. For secular theology the key word is identification. For me the key word is devotion. Indeed, the first fruit and the decisive mark of grace is "a sincere and pure devotion to Christ" (2 Cor. 11:3). Service in the world must be grounded in heartfelt devotion to the Savior, Jesus Christ. Ethical action cannot long maintain itself apart from spiritual passion.

I have chosen the term "devotion" rather than "piety" because the former term connotes a commitment of the will as well as an attitude of the mind. It must be recognized that devotion has a double meaning — adoration and commitment or consecration.

---

[15] Dietrich Bonhoeffer, *The Cost of Discipleship* (trans. Reginald Fuller), (London: SCM, 1959), p. 47.
[16] One of the signs of hope in conservative Protestantism is *The Reformed Journal*, edited by members of the Christian Reformed Church; it seeks to relate the gospel to all spheres of human life, including the economic and political.

My emphasis is on the second meaning — total commitment to Jesus Christ.

The necessity for devotion has been stressed by many theologians. Karl Barth states in *Evangelical Theology* that there can be no theology apart from devotion.[17] Bonhoeffer, who is the guiding spirit for many of the new theologies today, has affirmed: "Our hearts have room only for one all-embracing devotion, and we can only cleave to one Lord. Every competitor to that devotion must be hated."[18]

Devotion, it should be said, means the service of Jesus Christ, not simply worship. A devout person is a consecrated person, not simply a religious person. Devotion entails piety, that is, the fear of God, but it also includes mercy, service to our fellow humanity.

An evangelical devotionism must be grounded in the biblical message of the justification of the ungodly. Christ died for us while we were yet sinners — this was the fundamental doctrine of the Protestant Reformation. We are made acceptable to God not by our own holiness but by the alien righteousness of Jesus Christ. We are claimed by his love even though we deserve his condemnation because of our sins. Sanctification must follow justification, since God makes righteous those whom he declares righteous. Yet our sanctification is a lifelong process, and we are never fully cleansed of our sin while still in this mortal body. The carnal man is crucified in the decision of faith, but he is not yet eradicated. In contradistinction to Roman Catholicism and Eastern Orthodoxy, I hold to *simul peccator ac iustus* — the Christian is at the same time a sinner and righteous. But I also affirm that the sin of the Christian is behind him and that he is now on the way to being made righteous.

A second guiding principle of this theology is the necessity for Christian commitment. The justification that Christ procured for us by his death on the cross is only the beginning of our salvation; it is not the whole of salvation, as Barth sometimes insists. We are not yet saved until we lay hold of this justification in the decision of faith. God has acted decisively for our salvation, but we must respond to his saving offer even though we can do this only through his Spirit. Christoph Blumhardt expresses it tersely:

---

[17] Karl Barth, *Evangelical Theology* (trans. Grover Foley), (Garden City, N.Y.: Doubleday, 1964), pp. 75f.
[18] Bonhoeffer, *The Cost of Discipleship*, p. 157.

The crucified one, who is now the risen one, is the Lord. This we must believe. We have not gained much if we take it for granted that Christ died and rose again. Many people assume this and yet go into the path of hell. This assumption is of no use to me unless I make Jesus my Lord.[19]

Another salient mark of a theology of devotion is the call to the victorious life. Whereas the focus of attention in the old liberalism was upon the image of God in man and in the old orthodoxy upon the brokenness and helplessness of man, my emphasis is upon the new birth and the new life in the Spirit. Like the secular theologians I believe that the time has come for a new optimism, but this optimism must be grounded not in innate human powers but in the baptism and empowering of the Holy Spirit. Whereas Jesus was upheld as the prophet in the Social Gospel theology and as the mediator in neo-orthodox theology, I view Jesus primarily as the conqueror, the liberator. It is not the cross of Christ so much as the power of the risen Christ, the Spirit of Christ, that needs to be given special attention today.

The kingdom of God will also play a decisive role in this theology. I view the kingdom of God not as the reclaimed world, certainly not as the secular city, nor as the institutional church, but as the community of the redeemed, the remnant of the faithful. It is not enough to say that God's kingdom is where God reigns. God reigns over the entire universe, but his kingdom takes concrete form only where Christ is acknowledged as King. Reinhold Niebuhr has given prominence to the concept of the kingdom beyond history. This is a truth that must not be ignored, since the kingdom as a finished reality will indeed be completed only at the end of world history. Yet we must also hold onto another biblical truth, and that is that the kingdom is in the midst of the faithful, in the company of those who believe (Lk. 17:21). The kingdom is basically future, but it is already anticipated and mirrored in the children of light, those who are committed to Jesus Christ as Savior and Lord.

A final guiding principle of a theology of devotion is social relevance. Devotion to Christ must be expressed in the public as well as in the private areas of life. We cannot compartmentalize our religion; Christ is Lord of the whole of life. We cannot worship God

---

[19] R. Lejeune, ed., *Christoph Blumhardt and His Message*, p. 95.

on Sundays and yet remain silent when open villages are bombed in South Vietnam or when fruit pickers imported from Mexico are denied a living wage in California. At the same time this does not mean that Christian faith will ever be identified or conjoined with any social philosophy or ideology. The ultimate loyalty of the Christian is to a spiritual Lord, and this means that although he will serve in the world and sometimes even engage in political action, his motivations and goals will always be different from those of the man of the world. Sometimes the Christian will be politically to the right (when, for example, he enters the battle against pornographic literature), and sometimes he will be politically to the left (as, for example, in protests against weapons of mass extermination). But the Christian, that is, a person totally committed to Christ, will be intimately involved in the social and moral issues of the time. His goal will not only be individual piety but "social holiness" (Wesley).

The deepest affinities of a theology of devotion are to Lutheran and Reformed Pietism. Spener, Francke, Zinzendorf, and in more recent times Christian Spittler, Kierkegaard, and the Blumhardts also affirmed the need for personal devotion to Jesus Christ. Yet my position must not be interpreted as a neo-pietism, since many of my emphases are different, and I am speaking to a very different social situation. Whereas the early Pietists placed the accent upon the joys of the heart and the possession of salvation, my emphasis is on obedience and perseverance under the cross. For Pietism the new birth means peaceful possession and the enjoyment of salvation. I regard the new birth as a decisive commitment to the will and work of God. My focus is not upon the assurance of salvation but rather upon the working out of our salvation in fear and trembling. Like the Pietists I seek to relate the other-worldly to the this-worldly. The life of the Christian is to be centered in God, but he is called to live out his vocation in the world. Like such spiritual leaders as Spener and Zinzendorf, who in their time were ecumenical pioneers, I seek to overcome the barriers that have separated Christians through the ages.[20]

This position reflects some of the concerns of the later evangelical revivalism, but there are certain differences particularly from

---

[20] See A. J. Lewis, *Zinzendorf The Ecumenical Pioneer* (Philadelphia: Westminster, 1962).

revivalistic fundamentalism. My emphasis is upon a life of conversion, not upon a crisis experience of conversion (although there can be no obedience apart from experience). I seek an openness to the disciplines of the culture without utilizing them for apologetic purposes. Again I desire a faith that is biblical and evangelical without being biblicist. It is not simply the Bible as a book, but the paradoxical unity of the Bible and the Spirit that is the fundamental authority.

There are many who stand in the revival tradition who have successfully transcended a narrow biblicism. Christoph Blumhardt, who was nurtured in this tradition, affirms: "Our Bible is in heaven. Not one letter of it is of any use to me unless it is given from above."[21] And we would do well to pay heed to these words of William Booth, founder of the Salvation Army:

> Great as is the value of the Bible, it is possible to exalt it too highly. It is sometimes put in the place of God. The letter of it rather than its spirit has been held in chief regard. Others have made the mistake of regarding it as the only revelation God has made to the world. It contains the fullest and the clearest, but not the only, light He has given to men.[22]

Without denying the very solid contributions of neo-orthodoxy to theology today, I must also point to some basic areas of disagreement. In contradistinction to the general thrust of neo-orthodoxy I affirm that justification must be fulfilled in sanctification if it is to benefit us. I concur in the judgment of P. T. Forsyth: "He is not *for* us effectually till He is *in* us, He does not fully bless till He occupy us."[23] Also my outlook is dualistic rather than universalistic. I hold that devotion to Jesus Christ separates us from the world in its sin as well as identifies us with the world in its suffering. I believe that the kingdom of God is advancing in the world but that it holds sway only in the community of faith. The world as such still lies under the dominion of the evil one (1 Jn. 5:19). The elder Blumhardt was right

---

[21] R. Lejeune, ed., *Christoph Blumhardt and His Message*, p. 13.

[22] Cyril J. Barnes, ed., *The Founder Speaks Again* (London: Salvationist Publishing & Supplies, 1960), p. 202. One, of course, must go on to say that the biblical revelation is the final, definitive revelation of God and that all other light which God gives is an illumination and confirmation of it.

[23] P. T. Forsyth, *The Church and the Sacraments* (London: Independent Press, 1947), p. 242.

when he said, "Christ's victory remains forever sure; the whole world will be His!"[24] But the whole world is not yet his, just as the kingdom is not yet fulfilled. This means that my eschatology is radically futuristic, unlike that of many of the neo-orthodox theologians who hold to a realized eschatology. Jonathan Edwards well expresses my position: "It is needful that Christ should be the judge of the world in order that he may *finish* the work of redemption. It is the will of God that he who is the redeemer of the world should be a *complete* redeemer."[25]

My position has certain affinities with Roman Catholicism and Anglo-Catholicism in that it shares their concern with the life of devotion and consecration. Yet it contends that the saints are at the same time sinners and that the sacraments have no efficacy apart from the decision of faith. This view is genuinely catholic, although it is sometimes obscured by Roman and Anglo-Catholic polemicists. I see the place for ritual but not for ritualism; for the sacraments but not for sacramentalism; for Mary but not for Marianism; for the church but not for ecclesiasticism. I espouse an authentic Evangelical Catholicism, the kind represented by such theologians as Wilhelm Loehe, P. T. Forsyth, John Nevin, and Nathan Söderblom.

This position can also be called a Catholic Evangelicalism, which is to be distinguished from an ultra-conservative evangelicalism on the one hand and an ecumenical eclecticism on the other. We should not aim for the synthesis of Evangelical and Roman Catholic thought and practice but rather for their mutual purification in the light of the Word of God so that what is authentically evangelical and catholic might come to the fore.

THE ROAD AHEAD

Whither shall theology go as it faces an uncertain future? There are many voices calling the church in quite different directions. Some of these are the voices of false prophets, and a few others come from people illumined by the Spirit of God.

---

[24] R. Lejeune, ed., *Christoph Blumhardt and His Message*, p. 29.
[25] Jonathan Edwards, *Devotions of Jonathan Edwards* (ed. Ralph G. Turnbull), (Grand Rapids: Baker, 1959), p. 52.

Some voices are telling us that what is most essential is *restoration*. This is not in itself a bad emphasis, but it depends on what is meant by it. If it means that we must return to the "old-time religion" or to the Roman Catholic Church or to the confessions of the Reformation, then this smacks of archaism and reaction. What we should seek is a return to Jesus Christ, the living Word of God. Our concern should not be to recreate a golden age of the past but to spearhead the advance of the kingdom into the future. Theology must not return to an outmoded biblicism or an outdated sacramentalism; rather it must prepare the way for the advent of a biblical evangelical catholicism.

Other voices are calling the church to *renewal*. The influence of the new secular theology can especially be seen here. What too many people mean by this, however, is a renewal of social structures rather than a renewal of man. They speak of the promise of the secular city rather than of the new dispensation of the Spirit or the second advent of Jesus Christ. My position is that genuine renewal can come only by the Holy Spirit, and that all social gains will be cancelled unless they are grounded in and accompanied by repentance for personal and national sins.

Another party is contending that *revival* is the great need in our time. Insofar as revival predicates obedience to the will of God in all areas of life, this is a legitimate emphasis. If revival means simply being caught up in raptures and ecstasy, then we certainly need something more. Many of the new conservatives (including some Pentecostals) are pointing to the integral relationship of conversion and obedience in all spheres of life. Devotion to Jesus Christ has both a spiritual and an ethical dimension, and the latter must not be minimized.

Again there are voices calling for the *reformation* of the church. What is needed, these people say, are new forms and structures for Christian mission and service. There is much truth in this contention. The organizations of the local parish have by and large become outmoded and no longer serve the wider mission of the church. What we need are para-parochial groups, such as retreat houses and hospitality houses, as well as new forms of organization within the parish church. The local church should ideally be a lighthouse in a dark world, but where this is not possible or does not in fact take place, then new lighthouses should arise, never separated from the church but perhaps apart from the organizational machinery of the church.

Blumhardt pointed to the need for such centers of light:

> God always wants to have a place, a community, which belongs to Him really and truly, so that God's being can dwell there. God needs such a place from where He can work for the rest of the world. There must be a place on the earth from where the sun of God's kingdom shines forth.[26]

Yet no lighthouse can arise apart from personal repentance and conversion. This is to say that a reformation of the church will be useless unless it is basically a spiritual reformation, one that seeks for new persons as well as new forms and structures. What is called for is a purified church and not simply a reformed church.

Finally mention should be made of those whose primary concern is for *reconciliation*. This is another emphasis in secular theology; it also happens to be the theme of the Presbyterian Confession of 1967. In a time when races, churches, and nations are divided, there is indeed a crying need for reconciliation, for the tearing down of the walls which separate people from one another. Yet we must be reminded that there can be no social reconciliation apart from reconciliation between man and God. The vertical takes priority over the horizontal, and if man is alienated from God, he will be unable to overcome his alienation from his fellowman. Again I must insist that personal devotion to Jesus Christ is a prerequisite for becoming united in love with one's neighbor. This is to say that there can be no brotherhood of man apart from the Fatherhood of God and the Saviorhood of Christ.

At the same time we must not rest content with being in a right relationship to Christ and make no attempt to serve our neighbor for whom Christ died. Our devotion to Christ must be practical as well as spiritual, and this means that we must seek to bring the freedom and truth of Christ to all people. Again, Blumhardt's words are relevant: "What use is it to prattle about the kingdom of heaven if you leave your fellow men in their fetters and bonds, the slaves in their chains, and the oppressed in their misery?"[27] Blumhardt uttered what Catholic and Evangelical saints have always insisted —

---

[26] R. Lejeune, ed., *Christoph Blumhardt and His Message,* p. 81.
[27] *Ibid.,* pp. 64, 65

that faith in God must bear fruit in love to one's neighbor. Otherwise our faith is dead and our spirituality is a facade. May we seek to follow the Master out into the world, for it is there he beckons us. But may we not capitulate to the world, but rather wrestle with the principalities of the world, as did our Lord in the wilderness, and triumph over them through the power of his Spirit.

Three

THE CRISIS OF PIETY

IT CANNOT BE denied that modern Protestantism is troubled by
the demise of genuine piety. Theologians are now speaking of the
"crisis of piety" and the "loss of piety."[1] Indeed, the very term
piety has become opprobrious in modern religion and culture. The
radical criticism of the older piety and the quest for a new kind of
spirituality mirror a crisis of identity that presently afflicts Protestantism. Walter Wagoner contends that the dearth of piety is
especially noticeable in Protestant seminaries, which for the most
part have ceased to be "worshipping, praying communities."[2] He
states that such seminaries are refuges for many scholars who have
fled from the excesses of the older "pietism" and "have suddenly
discovered that most of their spiritual baggage was lost in the
flight."[3] In his view modern Protestant seminaries concentrate on
producing scholars of religion rather than persons of piety. Wayne
Oates refers to a "conspiracy of silence about personal religion" that

---

[1] See Edward Farley, *Requiem For a Lost Piety* (Philadelphia: Westminster, 1966) and
Edward W. Brueseke, "The Parish Ministry in a Crisis of Faith," *Minister's
Quarterly* (Fall, 1966), pp. 13-17.
[2] Walter Wagoner, "Winds and Windmills: A Weather Report on Seminary Educa-
tion in the USA," *Bulletin of the Department of Theology of the World Alliance of
Reformed Churches*, VI, no. 4 (Summer, 1966), p. 6.
[3] Walter Wagoner, *The Seminary: Protestant and Catholic* (New York· Sheed and
Ward, 1966), p. 51.

prevails in our theological schools and indeed in every area of contemporary church life.[4] George MacLeod has given this diagnosis of the religious situation: "The Church today is paralysed with self analysis. Its mission has become uncertain, its worship, still reverently respected, has lost its zest. . . . From the pulpit the trumpet sounds with an uncertain voice."[5]

THE MEANING OF PIETY

Piety in the Christian context essentially means heartfelt devotion and consecration to the God who has revealed himself in Jesus Christ.[6] It signifies the organizing pattern or style of Christian life, the way by which we seek to give concrete or practical expression to our faith. It involves a commitment that is total, one that affects every area of human life. There can be various types of piety insofar as certain elements of the gospel become the focal point of attention. Yet a piety that is grounded in Scripture will always be characterized by inward zeal or consecration, godly fear, and total dedication. Scriptural piety will be directed to the holy God incarnate in Jesus Christ. A piety that is directed solely to Jesus and not to Jesus Christ, the God-man, can only be regarded as a pseudo-piety. In Calvin's judgment: "True piety consists . . . in a pure and true zeal which loves God altogether as Father, and reveres him truly as Lord, embraces his justice and dreads to offend him more than to die."[7] Here it can be seen that piety is essentially a synthesis of the love and fear of God.

In the theology of the Reformation, piety was sharply distinguished from moralism, which signifies seeking to make oneself worthy in the sight of God. True piety presupposes a heartfelt conviction of one's own unworthiness before God and a sincere trust

---

[4] Frank Stagg, E. Glenn Hinson, Wayne E. Oates, *Glossolalia* (Nashville: Abingdon, 1967), p. 82.

[5] George MacLeod, "Nearing the Eleventh Hour?" in *The Coracle* (Dec., 1966), p. 13.

[6] The word "pious," which is related to the Latin *pius*, originally meant "careful of the duties owed by created beings to God." See *The Oxford Universal Dictionary*.

[7] John Calvin, *Instruction in Faith* (Philadelphia: Westminster, 1959), p. 19. This is the definition he gives in his *Institutes:* "I call 'piety' that reverence joined with love of God which the knowledge of his benefits induces." *Institutes of the Christian Religion* (ed. John T. McNeill; trans. Ford L. Battles), (Philadelphia: Westminster Press, 1960), I, 2, 1, p. 41.

and confidence in his mercy. Piety is grounded in and sustained by faith; it might even be considered the working out of faith to its fulfillment. It entails renouncing and denying the self and cleaving to Christ in repentance and devotion. But in the thought of the Reformers (particularly Calvin), piety also has another aspect — the pursuit of Christian holiness, a seeking after the perfection to which Christ calls us. In their view we cannot earn our salvation, but we should seek to uphold and confirm it in our lives. In this sense piety consists in the bearing of the cross after the example of Christ, an *imitatio Christi*. It was this aspect of piety that was especially pronounced in the later movements of Pietism and Puritanism.

THE PRESENT CRISIS OF PIETY

Modern sophisticated Christians are generally scornful of piety for various reasons. The confusion of piety and moralism in much current popular religion is undoubtedly one of the main factors in the demise of true piety. In culture religion, both in its liberal and fundamentalist guises, piety becomes a method of gaining self-fulfillment by means of spiritually significant activities. In the circles of popular orthodoxy, piety is often characterized by intro-version, the separation of the private and public spheres of morality. The reluctance of orthodox Protestants to speak out against social evils such as weapons of mass extermination and racial discrimina-tion in housing has brought the more conservative brand of piety into disrepute, particularly among intellectuals.

Neo-orthodoxy has contributed to the crisis of piety by placing the accent on what God has done for us in Jesus Christ and seemingly ignoring what we can do in and for Christ. The radical separation of divine revelation from religious experience has reinforced this devaluation of the subjective dimension of our salvation. Devotion or piety becomes significant mainly in relation to the subjective appropriation of our salvation in a Christian life. But in neo-orthodoxy the Christian life is regarded as only an effect or sign of the salvation gained for us once for all in Jesus Christ. As in the theology of the Reformers, the emphasis is on the justification of God, not the sanctification of man. Even Emil Brunner, who seeks to do justice to the subjective pole of salvation, minimizes sanctification. Karl Barth gives a much greater place to sanctification, but he describes it mainly in objectivistic terms — as something that happens to us in Christ. This is not to overlook Barth's very real concern for Christian discipleship and his call for a rediscovery of Zinzendorf, one of the guiding lights of Pietism.

The Holiness and Pentecostal movements have given new significance to the Christian life by maintaining that Scriptural holiness is not only possible but mandatory for every Christian in this life. Yet by confusing Scriptural holiness with entire sanctification or sinless perfection they have landed in the pitfall of perfectionism. There is a genuine zeal or devotion in these movements, but it rests partly upon the delusion that the Christian can somehow transcend sin. My objection to these movements is that they are not sufficiently penitential.

Finally the new secular or radical theology has done much to foster the disintegration of true piety by making the world rather than God the primary object of our concern. The arena of salvation is regarded no longer as the reconciling work of God in Christ on Calvary nor as the crisis of repentance and faith but rather as the present struggle for social justice. Jesus is upheld as the contagious model of human adulthood, but not as the Savior from sin. Prayer is understood not as dialogue with a personal God but as reflection upon the needs of our neighbor and then acting to meet these needs (J. A. T. Robinson, Paul Van Buren, Malcolm Boyd).

It must be recognized that the crisis of piety is directly related to the dissipation of faith and the growing secularization of modern culture. The weakening of faith has many causes, but certainly the deemphasis of the spiritual life in contemporary theology (both neo-orthodox and secular) is a contributing factor. Faith cannot live apart from prayer and devotion, and the church has not been able to fill this spiritual vacuum.

The new interest in counseling and group dynamics in our churches and seminaries mirrors an attempt to cope with the crisis of personal faith by encouraging people to turn inwards and discover who they are in relation to their God and neighbor. Yet too often a purely secular psychological perspective supplants a theological, biblical perspective, and our dependence is directed to our own latent powers rather than to the living Savior, Jesus Christ. It can be said that the fascination with psychotherapy in the religious world today reflects the modern cultural emphasis on self-fulfill-ment as opposed to bearing the cross, the mark of authentic piety. There is no wish here to denigrate the valid insights and findings in secular psychotherapy, but I question whether such insights can be the foundation for pastoral care or the cure of souls *(Seelsorge)*.

The liturgical movement has attempted to meet the crisis of piety by strengthening the services of worship and making the Eucharist central again in the lives of people.[8] This movement has much to commend it; yet there are many things in it that smack of aestheti-cism and archaism. The church today needs liturgical reform, but the answer to the problem of declining piety does not lie in formal prayers and litanies as such. People cannot be said to have personal devotion to Christ until they preach and testify with power and conviction and sing and pray from their hearts. The liturgical revival highlights rather than overcomes the crisis of piety.

This is not to deny that authentic Christian renewal will entail sacramental and liturgical renewal as well. Inward piety cannot maintain itself apart from external sacramental realities. Yet as P. T. Forsyth has reminded us, sacraments are only means, even though essential means. Our goal should be "sacramental souls" or "holy personalities."[9] It is fruits such as these that test the efficacy of our preaching and sacraments.

TOWARD THE RECOVERY OF PIETY

If piety means godly fear and devotion, then what is needed for its recovery is a renewed awareness of the transcendence and holiness of God. In popular Protestantism today, including the conservative variety, there is too much familiarity with God, a familiarity bordering on outright blasphemy. One cannot place absolute trust and fear in God who is only a fellow sufferer who understands (Whitehead). Neither can one truly fear a God who is only love and who is devoid of wrath and condemnation. The holiness of God can be properly grasped only in the light of the humiliation and death of Jesus Christ. The agonizing death of Christ on the cross attests to

---

[8] See "Appendix on Liturgical Renewal," pp. 143-147.
[9] P. T. Forsyth, *The Church and the Sacraments*, 2nd ed. (London: Independent Press, 1947), p. 141.

both the wrath of God against sin and his unfailing love for the sinner.

In this connection we need a new understanding of hell and damnation. One will not strive to work out one's salvation in fear and trembling if there is no divine judgment in the future, if there is no threat of condemnation. The reason why the traditional picture of hell has passed out of theological parlance is that it has been conceived in anti-Christian terms — as a place of torture, as separation from the love of God. What we must try to do is to perceive the wrath and condemnation of God in the light of his love declared in Jesus Christ.

Again, it is imperative that we recover the biblical understanding of prayer as petition and supplication. Apart from petitionary prayer there cannot be an evangelical piety. If Christians are at the same time sinners, Reformed theology maintains, then they will always approach the throne of God as suppliants. There may also be a place for mental or mystical prayer in the life of the Christian, but this must not be regarded as a higher form of prayer.

Finally, we need a fresh understanding of the decisive role of the Christian life in our salvation. Christian devotion or commitment becomes meaningless unless it is integrally related to divine justification and sanctification. The Christian life must be viewed as being something more than a by-product and sign of the salvation procured for us by Jesus Christ. It should be understood as the appropriation of this salvation in faith and love. Against the dominant strand of neo-orthodoxy I maintain that the locus of salvation is twofold — the cross of Christ and the obedience of faith. It is incumbent upon us to work out our salvation in fear and trembling because apart from the perseverance of faith salvation is forfeited.

The pious or godly person is one who seeks first the kingdom of God and the glory of God and yet who is also deeply concerned with his or her salvation. Indeed the paradox is that God is never more glorified than when his children seek to work out their salvation under the cross of Christ (cf. 2 Cor. 9:13). The glory of God is intimately related to the salvation of man.

It should be recognized that the key to the renewal of faith and piety in our time does not lie in a new theological understanding as such but rather in the outpouring of the Holy Spirit. The third-force Protestants are right in their emphasis upon the Spirit, but they err when they separate Spirit-baptism from conversion and seek for empirical evidences of the reality of the Spirit. Bonhoeffer has said that God must act in his own time before the church can again uphold the gospel before the world with power and authority.[10] Yet Christians can do much to prepare for the dispensation of the Spirit by a sincere repentance of personal and national sins and by concrete obedience to the will of God. And certainly the primal form of obedience is heartfelt prayer and the hearing and reading of the Word of God.

LEARNING FROM PIETISM

The post-Reformation spiritual movements known as Pietism, Puritanism, and Evangelicalism all sought to recover the centrality and priority of Christian commitment and devotion. That each one had marked limitations cannot be denied. The interiorization of piety, the idea that regeneration is accomplished in an experience of conversion, and the possibility of Christian perfection are commonly associated with one or another of these movements. It is not my purpose here to determine where they went astray but rather to discover what we can learn from them.

Whereas the Reformers place the accent upon *Christ for us,* these groups seek to give equal emphasis to *Christ with us* and *Christ in us.* The Pietist and revival theologians acknowledge that we are accepted while we are yet in our sins, but they point to the truth that God does not continue to accept us if we remain in our sins. While acknowledging the logical priority of justification, they remind us of its inseparable connection with sanctification. They concur in the judgment of the Reformers that God loves us as we are; but they go on to affirm that God wants us as he is.

The rediscovery of gospel evangelism is another note that can be appreciated in the movements of spiritual renewal, particularly Pietism and Evangelicalism. From their ranks came the great missionary expansion with Protestantism, and this is a fact that must not be lightly dismissed. The deep-rooted concern for the lost that motivated the evangelical revivalists is reflected in the motto of Zinzendorf: "My joy until I die: to win souls for the Lamb."

---

[10] Dietrich Bonhoeffer, *Letters and Papers from Prison,* p. 188.

Moreover, the revival movements were basically sound in their understanding of evangelism as the proclamation of the biblical message of salvation through the vicarious death of Jesus Christ and as the call to a decision of eternal significance. They remind us that salvation consists in the conversion of the whole person to the living Christ. What we must guard against is reducing the experience of conversion to any stereotyped pattern or form.

These spiritual movements also call our attention to the fact that there are two kingdoms locked in irrevocable warfare. I am not referring to the two realms — church and state — of Lutheran orthodoxy, but to the kingdom of God and the demonic kingdom of darkness. A theology of Christian commitment takes on new significance when this commitment is seen in terms of warfare against the demonic powers. This indeed is the theme of the theology of Johann Christoph Blumhardt, who was a noted healer as well as a charismatic preacher. To be sure the powers of darkness have been mortally wounded by the cross and resurrection victory of Jesus Christ, but they continue to wage war upon the children of light. The demonic is to be viewed not as an empty negation but as a power that is at the same time creative and destructive.

Again, we learn from such spiritual giants as Spener, John Wesley, Zinzendorf, and Richard Baxter that spiritual disciplines are very necessary in the life of the Christian. Such disciplines as prayer, devotional reading, and fasting are not to be regarded as means of earning our salvation, but they can be seen as aids by which we continue in the salvation purchased for us by Jesus Christ. They can be regarded as tokens of our gratefulness for the incomparable sacrifice of Jesus Christ. Albert Day rightly contends that the disciplines of the interior life are the lost dimension in modern Protestantism. It can be said that Christians today need to spend more time in the upper room and less time in the supper room.

We are also reminded that Jesus Christ is our pattern and example as well as our Savior. This note was not lost in the Reformation, but it became much more important in the movements of spiritual renewal subsequent to the Reformation. The *imitatio Christi* does not mean that we should copy Christ in externals, but it does mean that we should be conformed to his image in thought and work. This emphasis upon Christ as model and example can especially be seen in the writings of Kierkegaard, who had a basic spiritual affinity with Pietism and strongly reacted against the objectivism in Lutheran orthodoxy.[11]

Finally we can learn from these movements that *diastasis* (separation) is always necessary for the Christian. We hear much today of the necessity of being *for* the world, but Scripture also tells us that the church must be *against* the world as well. We must be for the lost and helpless in the world, but we must stand against the spirit of the world, the idolatry and sin of the world. The Christian life cannot exist apart from a certain degree of separation and withdrawal from the world. Even Bonhoeffer recognized this when he spoke of the need for an arcane discipline of devotion in the life of every Christian. Yet *diastasis* should not be practiced exclusively, because this would lead to ghettoism. What is called for is the dialectic of withdrawal and return, separation from the world and active involvement in the world.

A THEOLOGY OF DEVOTION

A theology of devotion or Christian life must be grounded in the doctrine of the justification of the ungodly if we are to avoid the peril of works-righteousness. Christ has justified us while we are still sinners — this is a truth propounded by Paul and reaffirmed by the Protestant Reformers. At the same time Christ also sanctifies us by his Spirit, and this is a truth we can learn from Pietism and Evangelicalism. We are not regenerated all at once at our baptism and conversion, but our regeneration has certainly commenced, and throughout our lives we can make real progress towards evangelical perfection if we abide in Christ.

The order of salvation *(ordo salutis)* will play a major role in any theology that seeks to take the Christian commitment with the utmost seriousness. It is fashionable in contemporary theological circles to speak only of various facets of the one great event of our salvation rather than of an order of salvation. Yet this kind of

---

[11] Kierkegaard has been designated as a child of Pietism by such scholars as Emil Brunner, J. Pelikan, and R. Gregor Smith. Brunner has maintained that the dialectical theology is indebted to two great figures of Pietism — Kierkegaard and Christoph Blumhardt. See his *The Divine-Human Encounter* (trans. Amandus Loos), (Philadelphia: Westminster, 1943), pp. 39, 40.

thinking fails to do justice to the biblical testimony that salvation has a definite beginning and that it progresses through a series of stages towards a final culmination.

I affirm that the Christian life plays a decisive role in the divine plan of salvation, although it is not its basis or source. Rather the Christian life is the arena in which our salvation is fought for and continually recovered. A life of devotion is not the foundation of salvation, but it is a vital element in our salvation. We are not justified by a Christian life, but we are sanctified through a Christian life.

A theology of Christian devotion will be oriented about the costliness of grace. Just as the grace of God cost the life of his own Son, so it must also cost us our comfort and security in this world. God's grace is free, but it is not cheap, as both Kierkegaard and Bonhoeffer recognized. This grace is given to us while we are still sinners, but it demands from us that we strive against sin and seek holiness in all manner of living (1 Pet. 1:15). In order to retain the grace of Christ we must take up our cross and follow him. Salvation is neither instant nor automatic. It involves a life of struggle and perseverance under the cross.

The new secular theology speaks of "servanthood" and "holy worldliness." The old orthodoxy placed the accent upon churchliness. I am calling for an emphasis on godliness or holy fear. There is much talk today of the need for becoming authentically human, yet, as John Chrysostom so poignantly stated, "To be a man is to fear God." The strategy that I favor is not withdrawal from the world into permanent seclusion but rather a hidden life of devotion held together with outgoing service to the outcasts and unfortunates in our midst. My motto is separation *and* identification. We are to be *in* the world but not *of* it (cf. Jn. 17:11, 14).

Yet I contend that devotion to God takes priority over charity to our neighbor. We are called to love both God and neighbor but to adore only God. Although Jesus had a strong healing ministry, he nevertheless withdrew to the wilderness for prayer even while crowds were seeking him to be healed of their infirmities (Lk. 5:15, 16). John Wesley distinguished between works of piety, which fulfill our duties to God and the church, and works of mercy, which discharge our obligations to our fellowman. In Wesley's theology the works of piety come first, although the two must always go together. Piety apart from mercy is piosity; mercy apart from piety is do-goodism.

The distinction largely inherited from Catholic mysticism and Protestant Pietism between the God-life and the good life (in the material sense) is now under criticism in various quarters. The Christian faith, secular theologians rightly contend, certainly supports the human quest for social justice and personal well-being in the world. Yet what must also be recognized is that there will always be a tension between the God-life and the good life. The Christian faith teaches self-denial before it speaks about self-fulfillment (Mt. 16:24, 25). Christians can hold the good things of life only as stewards (1 Cor. 7:25-31), and they must always be prepared to forsake these things out of loyalty to their Lord. Indeed it is precisely this readiness to forsake one's life for the kingdom that is the hallmark of discipleship.

A theology of the Christian life must be at the same time a theology of the Word of God. Indeed a life of faith and piety springs from the preaching and hearing of the gospel. In the last analysis no life however saintly can bring people the assurance of forgiveness they so desperately need. It is only when we are confronted with the message of salvation through the shedding of the blood of Jesus Christ that we are awakened to heartfelt faith and consecration. Life and word are organically related, and yet it is the Word of God that brings us the power to live a life of devotion and consecration.

This is not to deny, however, that works of piety and mercy can also be potent means of grace. To be sure they must be accompanied by the Word, and they must spring from the Word. Yet the Word of God does not take permanent root within us until we obey as well as believe. Faith apart from works is dead, and this means that our preaching is not effectual apart from a life of obedience under the cross. A theology of proclamation must be supplemented by a theology of devotion if Protestantism is to maintain itself in a secular age.

What is here proposed is a holiness in the world, a piety that is to be lived out in the midst of human suffering and dereliction. Such a holiness should be sharply distinguished from the other-worldliness of modern secularism and the ethereal other-worldliness of a certain kind of mysticism. Holiness is a gift of God, but it is also a goal that we are called to strive for in this world, in this life. We are summoned neither to separation from nor solidarity with the world but rather to combat with the evil forces of the world, and this means that the way of holiness is also the way of the cross.

Four

THE MISSION
OF THE CHURCH:
SPIRITUAL OR SECULAR?

CONTEMPORARY THEOLOGIANS ARE divided concerning the nature of the mission of the church. Conservative evangelicals and some Lutherans conceive of the church as having a purely spiritual mission. The new secular theologians envisage the church's mission as secular or this-worldly. They contend that the church exists not only wholly *in* but also exclusively *for* the world.

This debate also concerns the meaning and purpose of evangelism. The new secular theology conceives of evangelism in terms of political outreach and social action. The most potent kind of witness, according to Harvey Cox, may very well be marching on the picket line. Conservative evangelicals on the other hand see evangelism as the saving of souls. Barthian theology understands evangelism as the proclamation of a salvation already realized for all people in the life, death, and resurrection of Jesus Christ.

The kingdom of God is another area of controversy in modern theology. Cox and Winter see the dawning of the kingdom of God in the "secular city" or the "new metropolis." Karl Barth claims that the kingdom of Christ already encompasses the world, although the consummation of all things in the kingdom of God still lies in the future. Conservative Lutherans such as James Kallas envisage the kingdom of God in essentially other-worldly terms.[1] In the view of

---

[1] See James Kallas, *The Significance of the Synoptic Miracles* (Greenwich, Conn.: Seabury, 1961); see also his *The Satanward View* (Philadelphia: Westminster, 1966).

Jürgen Moltmann the kingdom is both radically future and this-worldly.[2]

The lines seem to be drawn between those who espouse the personal gospel of salvation from sin and those who contend for a new Social Gospel. The former conceive of the arena of salvation in terms of the crisis of repentance and faith; the latter maintain that the arena of salvation is none other than the present struggle for social justice and racial equality.

A SPIRITUAL MISSION IN THE WORLD

I maintain the mission of the church is essentially spiritual, since it concerns a kingdom whose origin and goal are in God.[3] Did not Jesus say that his kingdom is not of this world (Jn. 18:36)? Our chief purpose as Christians is not to build a this-worldly utopia but rather to herald the triumph of God over the kingdoms of this world. We are not to give glory to the creature, but rather we are "to glorify God and enjoy Him forever" *(Shorter Westminster Catechism).* And this God is the uncreated Spiritual Being who transcends, sustains, and judges the world.

Yet the spiritual mission of the church definitely has temporal implications and consequences. We are called to the service of God not in some other world but in the very midst of this world. It is incumbent upon us to live out our spiritual vocation in a secular context. We are bound to a spiritual Lord, but we should be intimately involved in the agonies and trials of our fellow human beings. Our lives are to be centered in God, but we are sent forth into the squalor of the world as his servants. We should not seek to escape from the temporal into the spiritual but rather to bring the spiritual to bear on the temporal. We are to live for the glory of God, but this entails seeking the total welfare of our neighbor. For God is never more glorified than when man gains freedom from all manner of evil. As Irenaeus put it, "The glory of God is man fully alive."

---

[2] Jürgen Moltmann, *Theology of Hope,* trans. James Leitch (New York: Harper, 1967).

[3] Whereas the secular might be defined as pertaining to life in this age or world (from *saeculum*), the spiritual is to be understood as referring to divine or heavenly reality. Just as the secular has to do with penultimate concerns, so the spiritual has reference to ultimate concerns, concerns that transcend this life and world. The Christian is directed towards the spiritual even while living in the secular.

But man is only *fully* alive when he has been born anew by the Spirit of God.

Christians will be both spiritual warriors and active participants in the secular world. Their underlying passion will be to uphold the eternal gospel of Jesus Christ, but they are also to have a lively interest in the society in which God has placed them. They will not necessarily repudiate the goods of this world, but seek to use them for the glory of the kingdom. They will be open to the secular but not wholly immersed in it, deeply concerned for it but not bound to it. Christians will live and work in the secular world, but they must take care not to become secularized, that is, preoccupied with the things of this world. They should accept that which is really creative and good in the world as a gift of God, but they must renounce the love of the world, which is the hallmark of secularism. It is well to pay heed to the words of Paul: "Do not be conformed to this world but be transformed by the renewal of your mind, that you may prove what is the will of God, what is good and acceptable and perfect" (Rom. 12:2).

In the deepest sense Christianity consists in the synthesis of the spiritual and the material, since the Word became flesh and dwelt among us. And yet the material is always subordinate to the spiritual in the Christian faith. The Word became flesh so that flesh might eventually be transformed into spirit. In the words of Athanasius: "He became man that we might become divine." The purpose of the incarnation of God is the "deification" of man. In Christianity the material is to be utilized for the glory of God but never to be idolized or sacralized. The children of Israel were permitted to take jewelry of silver and gold from the Egyptians, but they sinned when they used their gold to make a molten calf for the purpose of idolatrous worship.

Evangelism must be seen as the proclamation of the gospel for the salvation of all people. Salvation must not be confused with humanization or rehabilitation, as sociologists understand these terms. Rather it should be equated with justification and sanctification, and this means that it primarily concerns man's relationship not to society but to God. The Iona Community makes the distinction between "whole salvation" and "soul salvation" and upholds the former approach over the latter, which it associates with revivalism. This distinction is not valid, however, since when the Bible speaks of the salvation of man's soul it generally means the salvation of the whole man (cf. Mt. 16:26; Jas. 1:21; 1 Pet. 1:9). That Scripture speaks of the resurrection of the body testifies to the fullness and inclusiveness of this salvation. Yet the resurrection is an eschatological event and not a present demonstrable reality. Moreover, the body that is raised is a spiritual body (1 Cor. 15:44), and therefore once again we must speak of our salvation as "spiritual" rather than temporal or secular if we are to do justice to the biblical witness.[4]

Yet the mission of the church is certainly not exhausted by the concept of evangelism. We are called not simply to make converts but to make disciples, teaching them to observe all that Christ commanded (Mt. 28:20). It is imperative that we not only uphold Jesus Christ as Savior but also follow him as Lord. This means that our ministry will involve *didache* (teaching) and *diakonia* (service) as well as *kerygma* (proclamation). Since the convert cannot mature except in the community of the family of God, we need also to give serious attention to *koinonia* (fellowship).

It is well to bear in mind that the church must not only proclaim the good news of Christ's salvation but also prepare people to receive and continue in this salvation. We must minister to their bodily and emotional needs as well as to their specifically spiritual needs, since it is the whole person who accepts and obeys the gospel of Christ. Karl Rahner reminds us that "biological sustenance itself is in the service of the personal spirit of man, since the spirit, living a biological life, can only realize itself with the help of biological elements."[5] William Booth, founder of the Salvation Army, had as his motto "soup, soap, and salvation." He rightly saw that until people are given earthly bread, they are not able or ready to receive the Bread of Life. We must sometimes be Good Samaritans before we can be heralds. Yet, as our Lord reminds us, man cannot live by bread alone, but he depends for his very existence upon the word that proceeds from the mouth of God (Mt. 4:4). Our ministry is to

---

[4] In Luther's words: "Because flesh and blood cannot enter into the kingdom of God it must cease, die and pass away and rise in a new spiritual being in order to reach heaven." *D. Martin Luther's Werke* (Weimar: Hermann Böhlaus Nachfolger, 1909), XXXVI, 673 (trans. T. F. Torrance).

[5] Karl Rahner, *Theological Investigations* (trans. Kevin Smyth), (London: Darton, Longman & Todd, 1966), IV, p. 386.

the whole person, and for this reason it is geared to his or her eternal spiritual salvation.

Diakonia (service) is not merely a supplement to the spiritual mission of the church, but an integral element in it. We serve our fellow human beings with a supernatural love and for the purpose of preparing them for a supernatural kingdom. Our service is not to be confused with humanitarianism, which often takes the form of condescension and social uplift. We view our neighbor not simply as someone in need but as one for whom Christ died. We give ourselves to our neighbor because Christ first gave himself for us. We serve our neighbor because of our deep concern for his total welfare (both physical *and* spiritual). Only this kind of love is directed to the whole man; only this deserves to be called Christian love.

There is much talk today of helping the downtrodden and poverty-stricken. This is a concern that certainly belongs in the church, and yet we must insist that this kind of ministry should seek to alleviate not merely material but also and above all spiritual poverty. Indeed *diakonia* as well as evangelism must have for its final aim the conversion of human beings to God. St. Teresa put this very profoundly: "The soul of the care of the poor is the care of the poor soul."

Our service to our neighbor may very well involve social (that is, political) action, but this must not be equated with evangelism. Evangelism is directly concerned with the regeneration and redemption of a lost humanity. The immediate concern in social action is the fight against social corruption, not personal transformation. Moreover, social corruption can be curtailed but not eliminated, and then only by the force of law. Laws can restrain our rapacity, but they cannot make us better. Martin Luther King has stated that laws are necessary not to make bad people good but innocent people safe. We cannot build a perfect social order, but we can revamp imperfect societies in order to insure a wider degree of justice and a greater compliance with God's law. Calvin even believed that it is possible to organize a "holy community" — a temporal society in which every area of life is at least partly directed by Scriptural law.[6] Such a community presupposes conversion and

---

[6] In contradistinction to left-wing Calvinism I hold that the term "holy community" is better applied to the eschatological kingdom than to a church-state society. This kingdom to be sure is present in germinal form in the earthly church, but it will not be fully realized until the end of earthly history.

creates a climate where such conversions take place. Social action, however, does not in itself result in the conversion of souls and can by no means be a substitute for evangelism. As a general rule, churchmen but not churches should be engaged in specific programs of political action. The task of the church is to stir the conscience of the community so that men and women of every walk of life are awakened to the social evils that exist and are moved to courageous action.

It is necessary to make distinctions between the various modes of Christian service, and yet we must not lose sight of the truth that every Christian activity must finally be geared to bringing people closer to God. We can perceive this better in evangelism and *diakonia,* but our social action must also have this for its final goal even though its immediate concern is the rectifying of social wrongs. Both *diakonia* and social action therefore should prepare the way for evangelism, just as evangelism should bear fruit in social service. Certainly the primary mission of the church is to take the slums out of the hearts of people; yet if we are not at the same time concerned about taking people out of the slums we are preaching an introverted gospel and are blind to the fact that an individual is very much influenced by his social setting.

This brings us to the truth that the gospel we proclaim has both personal and social dimensions. It addresses itself to the injustices within society as well as to individual sin. Our preaching is to be prophetic as well as kerygmatic. The ambassador of Christ must call people and their communities to repentance. He also invites people into a new community apart from which they cannot have salvation. We enter the kingdom one by one, but we immediately find ourselves in the whole company of saints. We make our decision alone before God, but this decision cannot bear fruit except in the community of believers. Moreover, as members of the body of Christ we are now at war not only with the old man within us but also with the principalities and powers of the world.

We must not make the mistake of identifying the church or church-state community (Calvin's "holy community") with the kingdom of God. The church might be viewed as the kingdom in germinal form, and yet it is better to regard it as a vessel of the kingdom. The company of believers finds itself as a colony of heaven in a fallen world (cf. Phil. 3:20). We cannot build the kingdom of God on earth, but we can create centers of light in a world still under the immediate rule of the powers of darkness. We can set up signs and parables of the kingdom that is yet to come. This kingdom is now dawning, but it is yet to be established in power and glory.

The future kingdom is spoken of in the New Testament as a new earth as well as a new heaven. But it is well to remember that this is a transfigured or spiritualized earth. We are told that flesh and blood cannot inherit this kingdom (1 Cor. 15:50). In this new order there will be no marriage or giving in marriage (Mt. 22:30). Its temple or center will be none other than God himself, and God is a Spirit (Jn. 4:24).

THE TWO KINGDOMS

Lutheran orthodoxy conceived of two spheres — spiritual and temporal — which are correlated with church and state respectively. The Christian is a member of both spheres, and this means that he owes duties to each. This distinction is legitimate (cf. Rom. 13:1-7), but if it is pushed too far it tends to foster interiorized religion. It becomes particularly suspect when the temporal sphere is conceived of as a separate kingdom rather than the arena in which the Christian works out his salvation. Then the Christian is placed under two different standards of morality, a private and a public.

A different kind of error can be discerned in certain strands of modern theology (Barth, Tillich, Cullmann, Bonhoeffer) that include both church and state in the kingdom of Christ or the Spiritual Community. This view loses sight of the truth that God's kingdom is basically eschatological and that the forces of evil still exert real power in this world. God's kingdom is not simply the rule of God but also the realm where his rule is acknowledged.

The two kingdoms that Scripture speaks of are spiritual kingdoms — those of light and darkness (Col. 1:13; 2 Cor. 6:14, 15; Eph. 6:12). This world is a battleground on which these two kingdoms contend, and this warfare extends into the church as well as the state. The demonic powers have been dethroned by the cross and resurrection victory of Christ, but they continue to wage war. These powers must not be regarded as ministering or reconciled servants of Christ (as Cullmann maintains) but rather as hostile spiritual forces opposed to the rule of Christ, forces that have been mortally wounded but not yet vanquished. Indeed, the demonic realm becomes more destructive as the kingdom of God advances.[7] Every worldly state is either neutralized and restrained by the power of God or enslaved by the power of the devil. The church is where the victory of Jesus Christ is manifested, and yet even the church is constantly threatened by the kingdom of darkness. It can be said that the Inquisition and the Salem witch trials both signify the intrusion of the demonic into the institutional church.[8] Even those who remain faithful to Christ can be cast into prison by the devil (Rev. 2:10). It must be kept in mind that the devil's kingdom, unlike the kingdom of Christ, is transitory, and that although it wields great power it continues to exist only by God's permission.

This biblical perspective reminds us that the church is essentially an army, and that its mission is to drive out the demons from the lives of individuals and nations. Yet this warfare is spiritual, and our weapons are perforce spiritual (cf. 2 Cor. 10:3). Jesus was very insistent that his kingdom is not to be defended by the sword (Mt. 26:52; Lk. 9:54-56; Jn. 18:36). The sword of the Christian is none other than the Word of God. The dependence of the church is not on temporal or secular power but on the grace and love of Jesus Christ. This is very important in a time when the spiritual mission of the church is often made to serve purely temporal ends. We need think only of Cyprus where loyalty to the Orthodox faith serves Greek imperialism, or of the American South where religion is used to bolster the interests of the white ruling class. The truth that the strength of the church consists in vicarious love has been accepted by many of the leaders of the civil rights movement, who are moved by their Christian conviction to witness against social wrongs. Yet even in this movement religion is sometimes used as a cloak to further the pursuit of temporal power, in this case, "black power."

If we maintain that the church is a colony of heaven and that it serves a kingdom that is not of this world, then the church should

---

[7] Tillich, despite his attempt to deliteralize the demonic, has made this statement: ". . . with the increase of the power of the Kingdom of God, the demonic realm also becomes stronger and more destructive" (*Systematic Theology* [University of Chicago Press, 1957], II, pp. 163, 164). For Tillich the might of the demonic is broken only in principle by the cross of Christ.

[8] It is not the supposed presence of witches in Salem but the relentless persecution of afflicted and distraught people by church authorities that signifies demonism.

certainly not engage in partisan politics. It is ridiculous for the church as a church to declare itself on matters that are basically political and whose moral implications are not at all clear. I am thinking here of such issues as the admission of Red China to the United Nations or the suitability of presidential candidates. The confusion of the secular with the spiritual is rampant among the devotees of renewal activism.

At the same time I hold that the church must speak out on clear-cut moral issues, which very often are political as well or which may have political overtones. The evils of racial segregation, nuclear war, and sexual promiscuity and perversion are definitely censured by the Word of God, and the ambassador of Christ must preach against such evils out of spiritual conviction. (Indeed these evils can be regarded as spiritual as well as temporal.) He will be proclaiming the pure Word of God and not a political or sociological opinion, but this word definitely has repercussions in the secular realm. The error of some of those who have a conservative theological orientation is that they are reluctant to bring the gospel to bear on any social issue, and thereby tend to separate the spiritual and the temporal. The two must be distinguished, but they cannot be divorced. Whenever our neighbor is directly threatened by injury or death, then we are confronted with a spiritual issue. Berdyaev has rightly said: "Bread for myself is a material problem; bread for other people is a spiritual problem."

THE HOLY AND THE PROFANE

The bane of modern theology is that it makes no real distinction between the holy and the profane, the sacred and the secular. Schleiermacher wrote: "All that is human is holy, for all is divine."[9] The entire world is sacramental, according to Tillich, and in John Robinson's view even the sex act is spiritual or sacramental. The sex act at its best is fully human, but it is surely not divine. In Tillich's theology the holy is the depth of the common and is thereby present everywhere and in everything. Bonhoeffer protested against the separation of the natural and the supernatural, but he

---

[9] Friedrich Schleiermacher, *On Religion* (trans. John Oman), (New York: Harper & Row, 1958), p. 180.

never identified them.[10] Philip Micklem points out in his provocative book *The Secular and the Sacred* that when everything is sacred, then nothing is sacred. It is Eastern pantheistic mysticism, not Christianity, that identifies the holy and the profane.[11]

In biblical theology the Holy is none other than the presence of the living God who encounters us in Jesus Christ. The profane or the secular lies under the judgment of the Holy because of the sinful rebellion of the creature. Even the religious life of humanity stands under the judgment and censure of the Holy. The preaching of the Word and the sacramental acts of the church can be a vehicle of the Holy, but they themselves must never be equated with the Holy.

The church should not seek the sacralization of the profane but the turning of the profane in the direction of the Holy, the awakening of secular humanity to the reality of the Holy. The mission of the church is not to transform nature into supernature or the secular into the sacred, but rather to remind the secular that it exists under the judgment of the Holy and to bring secular humanity into the domain of the Holy.

The sacred-secular synthesis that many theologians seek can only be accomplished by an act of God. Indeed, such a synthesis will exist for the human community only "beyond history," in the coming kingdom of God. In the New Jerusalem we are told that there will be no temple because God himself will be the temple (Rev. 21:22). The tension and contradiction between the Holy and the profane will then not exist, since sin, death, and the devil shall have been conquered.

The mission of the church is becoming secularized today because we have lost sight of the spiritual mission of Jesus. It is to be acknowledged that this conception can easily become perverted, and yet we must not close our eyes to the truth that Jesus basically sought to bring people into communion with God. We need a fresh understanding of the purpose of the incarnation and of the eschatological character of the kingdom of God. We need to be reminded that Jesus did not come into the world to save sinners from oppression and persecution but from hell. Moreover, he did

---

[10] Bonhoeffer wrote: "And yet what is Christian is not identical with what is of the world. The natural is not identical with the supernatural or the revelational with the rational." *Ethics* (ed. Eberhard Bethge), (New York: Macmillan, 1965), p. 199.

[11] See Philip A. Micklem, *The Secular and the Sacred* (London: Hodder & Stoughton, 1948), pp. 57-59.

not come to save us for happiness and prosperity in this world but "for his heavenly kingdom" (2 Tim. 4:18). His intention was not to Christianize the structures of the secular city but to prepare people for the holy city, the New Jerusalem. Christ, to be sure, is the answer to our physical and material as well as our spiritual needs, although this answer cannot be seen in its full dimensions until the resurrection of our bodies. Indeed, we are told that if we seek first the kingdom of heaven the necessities of life will be given to us as well (Mt. 6:33).

It is interesting to note that Dietrich Bonhoeffer, who is regarded as the father of modern secular theology, held even toward the end of his career that the proclamation of the church is to be centered in the revelation of the holy God and not the problems of the mundane world. The church in his mind is to begin with God's holy Word and then to proceed to the world, not vice versa.

> It is necessary to free oneself from the way of thinking which sets out from human problems and which asks for solutions on this basis. . . . The solution of human problems cannot be the essential task of the Church. . . . The word of the Church is the call to conversion, the call to belief in the love of God in Christ, and the call to preparation for Christ's second coming and for the future kingdom of God.[12]

It is also imperative that we recover the biblical concept of the kingdom of darkness. It is well for us to bear in mind that the devil is called in the New Testament "the ruler of this world" (Jn. 14:30; 2 Cor. 4:4) and the "prince of the power of the air" (Eph. 2:2). The demonic is not to be understood as the secular but as the perversion of spirit that bends the secular to its purpose. It is the corruption not of the earthly but of the heavenly or angelic creation. Paul says that we are struggling not against flesh and blood but against "the world rulers of this present darkness," "the spiritual hosts of wickedness in the heavenly places" (Eph. 6:12). In the words of Forsyth: "It is with an organization, a conspiracy, of evil that we have to do, and not a mere bias. . . . The Lord has a controversy not with His people only but with a rival king and strategy."[13] The very purpose

---

[12] Dietrich Bonhoeffer, *Ethics*, pp. 356, 357.
[13] P. T. Forsyth, *The Church and the Sacraments*, 2nd ed. (London: Independent Press, 1947), pp. 96, 98.

of the incarnation is lost sight of unless we recognize a spiritual realm of darkness arrayed against the will and work of God. According to John: "The reason the Son of God appeared was to destroy the works of the devil" (1 Jn. 3:8).

We are presently confused concerning the mission of the church because we have demythologized the demonology of the Bible, and, as Kallas rightly points out, when demonology is cast aside eschatology soon follows. Indeed, demonology is an integral part of eschatology. We cannot speak of the culmination of God's victory unless we understand the meaning and purpose of this victory. The triumph of the kingdom of God is unintelligible if it does not entail the destruction of the kingdom of evil. The concepts of the church militant and the church triumphant lose their meaning if Christians are not engaged in a battle with the world rulers of this present age. May we seek to recover a truly biblical eschatology and commence to herald a kingdom that stands over against this world.

Five

TOWARD THE RECOVERY OF
THE DEVOTIONAL LIFE

M UCH OF THE discussion concerning Christian renewal today is geared in the direction of social and political action. The accent is upon involvement in the world. Bonhoeffer prepared the way for this new emphasis by his concepts of holy worldliness and religionless Christianity. It was Bonhoeffer who said that only by living completely in the world can one learn to believe.[1]

Yet there is another side to the Christian faith that also needs emphasis if authentic renewal is to come about in our time — the devotional or interior life. That there is a crying need for the recovery of the devotional life cannot be denied. If anything characterizes modern Protestantism, it is the absence of spiritual disciplines or spiritual exercises. Yet such disciplines form the core of the life of devotion. It is not an exaggeration to state that this is the lost dimension in modern Protestantism. There is a noticeable dearth of good hymns and sound books on prayer. The stress today is on Christian action and social relevance rather than piety.

Increasing numbers of theologians are beginning to question the loss of the disciplines of the spirit in the life of Protestantism. Albert Day has expressed the views of many dissidents:

---

[1] Bonhoeffer, *Letters and Papers from Prison*, p. 226.

We Protestants are an undisciplined people. Therein lies the reason for much dearth of spiritual insight and serious lack of moral power. Revolting, as we did, from the legalistic regimens of the medieval church, we have forgotten almost completely the necessity which inspired these regimens, and the faithful practices which have given to Christendom some of its noblest saints.[2]

Dietrich Bonhoeffer, despite his acceptance of the phenomenon of secularization, also decries the lack of discipline in modern Protestantism. He states that the principal malady of the modern church is cheap grace: the preaching of forgiveness without requiring repentance, baptism without church discipline, and communion without confession. In his book on evangelical community life, *Life Together,* he speaks appreciatively of the discipline of silence, the fellowship of prayer, and evangelical confession. In his *Ethics* he deplores "the inability of most Protestants . . . to understand the significance of such disciplinary practices as spiritual exercises, asceticism, meditation and contemplation."[3] Even in the final stage of his theological development he affirms the need for a hidden discipline of devotion that would preserve the mysteries of the faith from profanization. It is this side of Bonhoeffer that the devotees of renewal activism and secular theology have not sufficiently discerned.

Historic Protestantism has tended to regard the devotional life with suspicion partly because of the protest of the Reformation against works-righteousness. The Reformers, Luther and Calvin, inveighed against asceticism understood as a way of salvation. They reminded the Christian world of that time of the biblical truth that we are justified only by the alien righteousness of Jesus Christ. At the same time, spiritual disciplines were never lacking in their lives. They did not emphasize the devotional life, but the life of consecrated devotion was not the thing to be fought for at that time. Their theme was justification of the ungodly, although they also sought to make a place for the doctrine of sanctification. Calvin in particular tried to hold in balance the biblical truths of the justification of God and the sanctification of man.

---

[2] Albert E. Day, *Discipline and Discovery* (Nashville: Parthenon, 1961), p. 7.
[3] Dietrich Bonhoeffer, *Ethics,* p. 302.

It remained for the post-Reformation movements of Pietism and Puritanism to give proper attention to the interior life of devotion. The Pietists sought to carry through the Protestant Reformation by pointing to the need for a reformation in life as well as in doctrine. Spener maintained that only those are justified who are intent upon sanctification. In place of the legal obedience that he believed to be characteristic of Roman Catholicism he spoke of an evangelical obedience, which simply means lifelong fidelity to Jesus Christ. Out of Pietism arose the great missionary movements within Protestantism and also such charitable institutions as deaconess houses, church hospitals, epileptic homes, and church orphanages. The Pietists also made an outstanding contribution to hymnology. Puritanism was much more iconoclastic than Pietism regarding inherited forms of church worship and also much less removed from the political life of the time. The Pietists placed the accent upon the cultivation of the inner life whereas the Puritans sought to build holy commonwealths where every area of life would be under the rule of God.

The eighteenth-century movement in England and America known as Evangelicalism also had a high regard for the interior life. John Wesley attacked what he termed "solifidianism," justification by faith apart from works. In his opinion this was the bane of continental Lutheranism. Wesley remained true to the Reformation in his conviction that we are justified even while we are yet in our sins. At the same time he maintained that we are not fully saved until we are cleansed of our sins. Like Spener he pointed to the indispensability of evangelical obedience and personal holiness. Wesley also spoke of the need for spiritual disciplines including fasting, prayer, confession of sins to one another, and devotional reading.

It can be seen that the life of consecrated devotion has had an important place within Protestantism. Now, however, piety is a term of ill repute. Discipline is seen more in terms of punishment than of training by modern Protestants and also by modern culture. Asceticism is associated with world-denial, and is thereby regarded with disfavor by most Protestants, even those who are conservative and orthodox theologically.

What is needed is a rediscovery of the biblical meaning of asceticism and discipline. Asceticism as a method of salvation or as a renunciation of the world for the purpose of finding inner peace must of course be opposed. Yet although the Bible teaches the acceptance of the world as God's creation, it strongly insists upon the denial of the self. Asceticism can be accepted if it is viewed as training to mastery over the passions. Paul called upon his hearers to mortify their flesh and to die to the self (Rom. 8:13; 1 Cor. 3:3; Gal. 5:16-24). By the "flesh" he meant the perverse element within us and not merely our physical appetites. He wrote to the Corinthians: "I pommel my body and subdue it, lest after preaching to others I myself should be disqualified" (1 Cor. 9:27). We cannot earn or merit salvation by means of spiritual exercises, but we can in this way strengthen ourselves for Christian service. We cannot justify ourselves by a disciplined life, but we can make progress in our justification by such a life. Calvin affirmed that we are justified not by works and yet not apart from works.[4] The works of faith and loving obedience do not procure the grace of God, but it is only through such works that his grace is operative in our lives. We receive the grace of God apart from any effort or merit of our own, but we do not continue in grace unless we strive to work out our salvation in fear and trembling. The necessity for constant wrestling and striving is underscored by the apostle: "Strive for . . . the holiness without which no one will see the Lord" (Heb. 12:14).

Dangers in Spiritual Disciplines

In our attempt to reinstate spiritual exercises we must be aware of the dangers in such an enterprise. We can learn from our Reformation forebears that a lively interest in spirituality can have dire consequences unless it is securely grounded in the Word of God.

One danger that we must guard against is moralism, the attempt to make oneself worthy in the sight of God. The disciplines of the spirit then become means of winning or earning our salvation. These disciplines must not be regarded as meritorious; rather they should be seen as having practical value. They strengthen us in faith and ongoing sanctification. They are the cause neither of justification nor of sanctification. Rather they are the fruits of God's favor toward us and the means by which we lay hold of the riches of God's mercy.

---

[4] Calvin, *Institutes* (McNeill ed.), III, 16, 1, p. 798.

Another peril in the spiritual life is escapism. The disciplines of the spirit then become means by which we seek to lift ourselves above the world or withdraw from the wider society into a private world of contemplation. The tradition of dualistic asceticism in Christian history has fostered escapist religion. This is the kind of asceticism that seeks to extricate spirit from the bonds of nature. It has its source in Neo-Platonism and Manichaeism and entered the church by way of the Christian mystics. The spiritual disciplines are not to be seen as a pretext for separation and isolation from the world. Rather they should be regarded as a means to conquest over the world. Not the renunciation of the world but service in the world — this is the purpose of the disciplines of the spirit as seen in the Bible. The inner-worldly asceticism of left-wing Calvinism is closer to the biblical idea than an asceticism rooted in a metaphysical dualism. The Puritans sought not to renounce the good things of life but rather to utilize these things for the glory of God. It was their intention not to escape from the world but rather to bring the world, indeed, every area of life, under the rule of God.

It must be recognized that within the mystical and ascetic tradition of the Christian faith there have been many examples of self-giving service in the world. It should also be admitted that there is a mystical element in the Christian faith itself that is not sufficiently discerned by either neo-orthodox or secular theologians. The mystical experience of the living God might be regarded as the subjective pole of revelation. We are in the camp of mysticism and spiritualism only if we fall into the error of viewing this experience as the exclusive and final criterion for truth.[5] The mystical element should always be conjoined with the historical revelation recorded in Scripture if the perils of introversion and escapism are to be avoided. Our trust should be placed not in the mystical vision or the inner light alone, but also and above all in the Christ of the Scriptures who calls us to obedience in the world.

Undoubtedly another temptation of the spiritually disciplined person is Pharisaism, the pretense of being more spiritual than one really is. The Pharisee places the emphasis on outward show, but often lacks the inward spirit of love. He practices spiritual disciplines mainly to impress others with his own holiness. What

---

[5] Mysticism refers to direct inward communion with God, whereas spiritualism signifies the belief that truth is located in the inward Spirit or inner light.

characterizes the Pharisee is not sanctity but sanctimoniousness. His abiding sin is that he trusts in himself that he is righteous and despises others (Lk. 18:9). He pretends to see, and this is why he is ultimately rejected by Christ (Jn. 9:39-41).

Closely related to Pharisaism is perfectionism. This might be defined as the belief that everything that Christ demands of us can be and sometimes is attained in this life. Spiritual disciplines become tools by which we supposedly enter into Christian perfection. Christian perfection is indeed the ultimate goal of the Christian, and yet it is not fully attainable in this life. It is well to bear in mind that Christ calls us to absolute perfection, and this means a state of perfect love comparable to that which characterizes God himself (Mt. 5:48). We can attain a measure of perfection but not perfection itself. We can keep the law through the grace of God, but we cannot fulfill the law. We can have freedom from every particular sin; yet we cannot be totally free from the presence of sin. Spiritual disciplines are necessary to keep us on the path to Christian perfection, but they cannot procure this perfection. Wesley rightly maintained that final holiness is a gift of God just as is justification itself. It is tempting for consecrated Christians to believe that they have arrived at the perfection Christ demands, that they are now in a state of entire sanctification or sinless perfection. But the Scripture tells us that no person is without sin (Ps. 14:3; 53:3; Rom. 3:10-12, 23; 1 Jn. 1:8). Indeed, even our most lofty desires and virtues are tainted by sinful pretension. This is why we must repent of our virtues as well as of our vices. We must repent of our imperfect self-discipline as well as our sins.

Finally we must give some attention to the heresy of rigorism, which might also be termed rigoristic legalism. This kind of thinking makes rigid adherence to law a precondition for salvation. The disciplines of the Christian life become inflexible standards. Spiritual exercises become oppressive rather than liberating. We should understand such exercises not as laws but rather as practical aids and guides to Christian living. The Christian is a free person and is not absolutely bound to any discipline or law except the word of the living God which is roughly identical with the law of love. Spiritual disciplines must always be viewed as voluntary, never as compulsory. Moreover, our trust should be not in our own striving but in the grace of God. The Methodist theologian W. E. Sangster has rightly said that Christian discipline is "not the toilsome, straining, failing effort to be good; but the faithful attending on God to receive."[6]

TYPES OF SPIRITUAL DISCIPLINE

When we think of spiritual disciplines the one that most often comes to mind is prayer. Indeed apart from prayer no other discipline has any spiritual or practical efficacy. Prayer is the very soul of faith (Calvin). It is "the sovereign remedy" for every kind of ill (Francis de Sales).

By prayer I do not mean reflection upon the needs of our neighbor (Van Buren, J. A. T. Robinson) nor meditation upon the ground of being (Tillich). Prayer in the biblical sense consists in heartfelt conversation with God as Personal Spirit. Too many manuals on the devotional life define prayer as a state of wonder or contemplation. True prayer is dialogue between the holy God and man the sinner. Prayer is essentially petition, since man always comes before God as a suppliant.

Prayer is a gift of God, but it is also a task or exercise of man. This is why prayer can be regarded as one of the spiritual disciplines. Calvin recommended prayer before work in the morning, before and after meals, and before bedtime. Luther suggested that in our prayers we make use of such objective symbols as the sign of the cross. Spener advocated keeping prayer lists for the purpose of daily intercession. A prayer room — a special room in the house set aside exclusively for the purposes of prayer and meditation — can be recommended as an aid for private prayer.

Although prayer and meditation must not be confused, meditation rightly understood also has a place in the Christian life. Paul calls us to set our minds on things above (Col. 3:2) and to think about those things that are true, honorable, just, and pure (Phil. 4:8). Meditation is not to be regarded as a higher form of prayer than supplication, but it can be viewed as a preparation for true prayer. Meditation or mental prayer has been much more emphasized in Roman Catholic and mystical circles than in the churches of the Reformation. One reason for this is that the Reformers were

---

[6] W. E. Sangster, *The Path to Perfection* (New York: Abingdon-Cokesbury, 1943), p. 197.

particularly insistent upon prayer as dialogue and not silent contemplation; at the same time they recognized the rightful place for meditation on the themes of the Bible. Luther in particular stressed the need to meditate constantly upon the passion of Christ. One of the saints of the Scottish church, Henry Scougal, has written: "This mental prayer is of all others the most effectual to purify the soul, and dispose it unto a holy and religious temper, and may be termed the great secret of devotion and one of the most powerful instruments of the divine life. . . ."[7]

Study of the truths of the faith is still another discipline that should be practiced by all Christians. Ministers today find it difficult not only to maintain the arduous work of prayer but also the discipline of study. It is an open scandal how few ministers read serious books in theology (let alone devotional books) after their graduation from seminary. Study is, of course, a discipline incumbent upon all Christians, not just the clergy. The motto of the Christian faith is in Anselm's words "faith seeking understanding," and this entails rigorous study not only of the Bible but of doctrinal and devotional works as well. Some of the spiritual masters have suggested setting aside Sunday as a day for serious reading of the Bible. Every Christian who knows how to read and write can do this much for the kingdom of God. On the matter of extrabiblical reading lay people should be advised to go to the spiritual classics first and then to more doctrinal writings. Unfortunately many pastors are introducing their lay people to such books as *Honest to God* and *The Secular City*, but neither of these can be considered a spiritual classic.

Family devotions are also very much neglected in modern secular Protestantism. The publication by denominational agencies of devotional booklets often containing short articles by theologically unqualified persons has not remedied the situation. What is needed is a rediscovery of the devotional classics on the part of modern Christians, particularly Protestants. One recommendation is that Scripture be read following table grace at every meal. Another is that the various members of the family take turns in reading selections from one of the devotional classics after the evening meal. The singing of hymns either at mealtime or on Sunday afternoons or

---

[7] Henry Scougal, *The Life of God in the Soul of Man* (ed. Winthrop S. Hudson), (Philadelphia: Westminster Press, 1948), p. 92.

evenings is another spiritual discipline that can contribute much to a united family witness for Jesus Christ.

Simplicity is yet another discipline of the spirit which can be held up to Christians, particularly to those who live in our affluent society. One should not try to appear younger, wiser, or richer than one is (Albert Day). As Paul said, "Love makes no parade, gives itself no airs" (1 Cor. 13:4, Moffatt translation). We are told that Christian women should adorn themselves modestly and not with costly attire (1 Tim. 2:9). In a time when millions dwell in nearly total poverty, Christians, especially ministers of the gospel, should not seek to live in luxury. In our culture, with its stress upon the accumulation of material goods, we need to remind ourselves that most of these things are unnecessary and time-consuming. Christians should not renounce the goods of the world, but they also should not burden themselves unduly with these things. Nor should they seek for these goods before they seek for God.

Closely related to simplicity is the discipline of fasting. In a time when one of the dominant sins in America is gluttony, it is salutary to do without food for short periods in the year in order to draw close to God in prayer. Fasting also sets us free for service to our neighbor. By skipping a meal every now and then, we can use this time to visit or pray for the sick; the money that we save can be used to help someone in dire distress. Fasting can be recommended particularly during Lent, when we are called to make a special effort to meditate upon the passion of Jesus Christ. This discipline was held in high esteem by Luther, Calvin, and Wesley. In our day it has been strongly advocated by Bonhoeffer.[8] When our part of the world is eating itself to death while the other two-thirds are starving to death, we need to bear in mind the spiritual significance of fasting. Fasting is, of course, not dieting, but it is an identification with those who have no means of sustenance. When fasting becomes normative or fashionable, then obviously it can no longer be considered a work of piety. But to fast and pray in secret — this is the way of Christian discipleship.

Chastity is a discipline that should also be given special consideration. In a time when there is an almost complete breakdown of sexual mores in our society, it is well to take note that Jesus Christ

---

[8] Dietrich Bonhoeffer, *The Cost of Discipleship*, pp. 151-153.

calls every Christian to a life of chastity. We are told that adulterers, homosexuals, and fornicators will be barred from the kingdom of heaven (1 Cor. 6:9, 10; Rev. 21:8). Chastity does not necessarily imply virginity and celibacy, as a dualistic asceticism would have us believe. Chastity as a spiritual discipline means abstinence from sex apart from marriage and temperance within marriage. This may seem an almost impossible task for many people, and yet this ideal can be approximated and even realized through the grace of God. Chastity may in some cases imply permanent abstinence from sex but only for the purpose of greater freedom for service in the kingdom.

Another kind of asceticism that should be considered is abstinence from liquor and tobacco. If such renunciation is undertaken voluntarily and if it is done for the purpose of strengthening ourselves and others in the service of Christ, then it is something to be encouraged. The ravaging disease of alcoholism is now a major peril in America and in some other Western nations including France, Italy, Denmark, and Sweden. The startling rise of lung cancer in modern civilization can now be shown to be directly correlated with the sale of cigarettes. It is therefore wise to abstain from intoxicating drinks and tobacco not in order to make ourselves virtuous but rather to protect our bodies, which are the temples of God, and to help our weaker brethren who need to abstain if they are to survive in the kind of culture in which we live (cf. Rom. 14:21; 1 Cor. 8:13). Wesley recommended abstinence from liquor but only as a voluntary discipline. When such disciplines are practiced in order to gain spiritual merit or social standing, then they become instruments of legalism and Pharisaism. It is well to bear in mind that Jesus himself did not abstain from wine, although one should recognize that he was living in a culture in which drinking was tightly controlled by religious sanctions, and alcoholism was not a real problem. Temperance, not abstinence, is of course the Christian ideal, but abstinence should be encouraged in those societies that are internally threatened by profligacy and alcoholic addiction.

The discipline of Sabbath rest needs to be emphasized in our day The desecration of the Christian Sabbath is becoming ever more scandalous, and yet only a few of the smaller denominations take a stand on this problem. I am not advocating blue laws (although such laws may have a place in some communities), but I am urging

Christians to dedicate themselves in a special way to the service of God on the Sabbath. This is a day that should be given over to hospitality, visits to the sick, and spiritual reading. We are called to rest from our worldly labors on the Lord's Day, but following the example of Jesus we should then labor for the kingdom.

Finally, we should give some attention to the discipline of partaking of the Lord's Supper. It may seem surprising to speak of this as a spiritual discipline, and yet Holy Communion must be sought for ever again if we are to grow in the spiritual life. Such masters of spirituality as Thomas à Kempis and Martin Luther regarded the Blessed Sacrament as a veritable means of grace, a necessary aid to sanctification. In the words of St. Ambrose: "Because I always sin, I am always bound to take medicine." The hearing of the Word of God in church is certainly one source of the medicine of grace, but participation in the sacrament is definitely another. Many writers on the spiritual life especially within Protestantism neglect this particular discipline, and this is only another sign of the loss of catholic substance in our churches.

There are other spiritual disciplines that could be mentioned such as tithing, hymn-singing, private confession of sins, early rising, and silence. The important thing to remember is that not every spiritual discipline is suitable for all Christians. Spiritual exercises must be voluntarily undertaken, and they must be abandoned once they have outlived their usefulness. Just as athletes need to proceed from one exercise to another in order to excel in their particular field, so Christians need to practice a variety of spiritual exercises if they are to run the race of life successfully.

RECOVERY OF THE DEVOTIONAL LIFE

As has been said, spiritual renewal in our time is linked to the recovery of the devotional life. Christians, particularly Protestants, need a new appreciation and understanding of the doctrine of the saints. We need to be reminded that the New Testament speaks not only of a holy gospel but also of a holy people. If the church is to maintain itself in a secular age it must again sound the call to consecrated devotion and holiness. It must place the accent not upon organizational efficiency but rather upon the spiritually disciplined life. Only in this way will it avoid a total capitulation to the culture.

At the same time, Protestants should beware of imitating Catholic practices of devotion and spirituality. Much Roman Catholic (and also Eastern Orthodox) spirituality is grounded in the dualistic asceticism criticized above. What we should aim for is an evangelical spirituality, one that is based upon salvation through the free, unmerited grace of Jesus Christ.

Yet this does not mean that we should ignore the very real contributions of the Catholic church through the ages. There is much genuine sanctity in the Roman church, and this communion continues to produce saints who are worthy of emulation. Moreover, Catholic theologians are now reappraising the meaning of sainthood and seeking to bring this doctrine more into accord with Holy Scripture. Ida Friederike Goerres in her book *The Hidden Face* shows how one of the modern saints, Thérèse of Lisieux, completely overcame the doctrine of merit and demonstrated a life of self-giving that was fully anchored in the Scriptural message of free grace. Such theologians as Hans Küng and Thomas Merton also seek to reinterpret the doctrine of holiness in the light of the gospel.

My position is that the devotional life if it is to avoid the Charybdis of legalism and the Scylla of spiritualism must be solidly anchored in the message of the Protestant Reformation. Devotion cannot be elevated above doctrine if we are to remain true to the deepest insights of the Reformers. It was Luther who said: "We can be saved without love and concord . . . but not without pure doctrine and faith."[9] This statement is abhorrent to many devout people, but it contains the truth that our love however necessary is never perfect in this life and therefore cannot save us. Our faith however imperfect is absolutely essential for laying hold of the riches of God's mercy, since faith simply means cleaving unto the righteousness of Christ. In the final analysis the most potent means of grace is the Word of God, not lives of selfless dedication under the cross. It is the death of the Son of God on the cross, not the bearing of the cross by Christians, that has procured our salvation. The Christian life can also be a means of grace, but only when it is informed by the message of salvation through the blood of Jesus

---

[9] Jaroslav Pelikan, ed., *Luther's Works* (St. Louis: Concordia, 1964), XXVII, p. 41.

Christ. And even then the life of the Christian falls short of the perfection to which Christ calls us. Fénelon, who sounded the call to Christian perfection, could nevertheless exclaim: "Even the good are only half-good, and make me groan almost as much as the others."[10] Perhaps the Reformers erred by placing so much emphasis on right doctrine and by not speaking enough of the need for a reformation of life as well. And yet there is truth in their message that must never be lost, namely, that only by faith are we declared righteous and then not because of our merits but solely because of the mercy of God in Jesus Christ.

The motivation for living the Christian life in evangelical theology is none other than the love of God born out of gratefulness for what he has done for us in Jesus Christ. There are other motivations that are also legitimate, such as the seeking for salvation and the fear of God. Yet the prime motivation for evangelicals is simply the desire to glorify God in everything we say or do. The purpose of a disciplined life is not to win special merits for ourselves or to gain a reward in heaven. Rather it is to make ourselves ever more free to bear witness to the One who saved us from sin, death, and hell. It is to enable us to live ever more fully for the glorification of God and for the salvation of humankind. What is needed in our time is a spiritual awakening that will drive us to our knees in repentance for personal and national sin. And then filled with the Holy Spirit and a renewed assurance of our salvation we can rise again to live and die for the glory of God.

---

[10] François Fénelon, *Christian Perfection* (ed. Charles Whiston; trans. Mildred Stillman), (New York: Harper, 1947), p. 125.

Six

THE MEANING
OF CONVERSION

C ONVERSION IS AGAIN becoming a live issue in theology. The
new interest in the Christian life and the sacraments has
focused attention upon the meaning of the decision of faith. The
growing ecumenical dialogue has also served to awaken interest in
the doctrine of conversion, inasmuch as soteriology has been the
principal area of conflict between Catholicism and Protestantism in
the past.

The English word "conversion" is associated with the Hebrew
word *shuv,* which means to turn back or return, and the Greek
words *epistrepho* and *metanoeo,* both of which indicate to turn
toward God. The key term in the New Testament is the latter,
together with its noun form *metanoia.* This term signifies not simply
a change of mind (as in classical Greek), but a change of heart.
Metanoia can also be translated as "repentance." John Wesley was
certainly true to the basic witness of Scripture when he defined
conversion in his dictionary as "a thorough change of heart and life
from sin to holiness, a turning."

Conversion was a key concept in the psychology of religion that
flourished in the first part of the twentieth century. William James
defined conversion as the process, gradual or sudden, by which
a self that has been divided becomes unified and happy as a

consequence of its firmer hold on religious realities.[1] It is the kind of process that is accessible to empirical investigation. My objection to this view is that it loses sight of the spiritual dimension of conversion. Conversion is not a "psychic" event but a miracle of grace. It originates not in the psyche but in the Spirit of God. Although the fruits of conversion, such as love and joy, are open to psychological study, the event itself is hidden from the eye of the natural man.

THE CONTEMPORARY DEBATE

The doctrine of conversion has become a matter of controversy in three principal areas: the relation between divine grace and human freedom; the locus of conversion; and the scope of conversion, to what extent it influences the secular life of man.

The contemporary Catholic-Protestant dialogue has compelled theologians to reassess the theological conflicts at the time of the Reformation and to determine whether we have actually moved beyond this cleavage. Catholic theologians who have sought to give a fresh restatement of the soteriological problem are Hans Küng, Karl Rahner, and Louis Bouyer; among Protestant thinkers addressing themselves to this debate are Karl Barth, G. C. Berkouwer, Rudolf Ehrlich, and Arthur Crabtree.

It seems that Catholic theology continues to speak of universal prevenient grace, by which man is enabled to cooperate with God and thereby obtain justification. In this view man's conversion, which is brought about by cooperation with infused grace (gratia infusa), is the basis of his justification. Justification is a confirmation of that which has already taken place, the inner renewal of man. In the Protestant view, superbly enunciated by Ehrlich in his book Rome: Opponent or Partner?, justification is an imputation of righteousness to those who are not deserving and is not contingent upon our inner renewal, although the latter invariably follows from the former.[2] Küng, in seeming contrast to the dominant strand in Catholic theology, argues that justification is prior to regeneration

---

[1] William James, The Varieties of Religious Experience (New York: Collier, 1961), p. 160.
[2] See Rudolf J. Ehrlich, Rome: Opponent or Partner? (Philadelphia: Westminster, 1965).

and is indeed the foundation of regeneration or conversion.[3] Ehrlich contends, however, that Küng still speaks of justification as being appropriated by faith understood as positive yearning and incipient love and that he thereby continues to make a place for human cooperation in salvation. Faith, according to classical Protestant theology, is an empty vessel and contributes nothing itself to our justification.

Bouyer accuses Protestant theology of holding to what he calls "extrinsic justification," which means that man is declared righteous without also being made righteous.[4] This seems to be a misunderstanding of the Reformation position, since both Calvin and Luther held that justification, although essentially the verdict of divine acquittal, leads to man's inner renewal by the Spirit of God. For Calvin justification and sanctification are to be distinguished, but they must never be separated. Justification as divine acquittal is extrinsic to man, but the fruits of this justification are then applied to man by the Holy Spirit. Bouyer's criticisms seem to have more merit when applied to neo-orthodox theologians such as Barth and Ehrlich. According to these men we can only acknowledge the justification that has already taken place in Jesus Christ. Yet even they do not deny that there is an inner renewal which is realized in faith, although they insist that we are justified even apart from such renewal. For the Protestant Reformers the Spirit must seal the justification of Christ in the hearts of people if they are to be truly justified.

For Reformation and neo-Reformation theology man cannot of himself lay hold of his justification, since his will is bound to the power of sin. Whereas Catholic theology maintains that the freedom of the will is not extinguished by sin, Protestant theology holds to the spiritual bondage of the will. This is why we stand in need of radical conversion; our will must be turned from the pursuit of power to the service of God. But only the Spirit can effect the

---

[3] Although Karl Rahner is basically sympathetic to Küng, he contends that we are justified by love as well as faith. Rahner refuses to draw any basic distinction between justification (in its subjective mode) and sanctification. See his "Questions of Controversial Theology on Justification," in his *Theological Investigations*, IV (trans. Kevin Smyth), (Baltimore: Helicon, 1966), pp. 189-218.
[4] Louis Bouyer, *The Spirit and Forms of Protestantism* (trans. A. V. Littledale), (Westminster, Md.: Newman, 1961), pp. 139f.

revolution of our will; only the Spirit can set us free to respond to the offer of salvation.

A second area of controversy in modern theology concerns the locus of our conversion. Granted our dire need of conversion, where does this conversion take place? Karl Barth maintains that our conversion has already taken place in Jesus Christ in that he as the Representative Man died once for all to sin and rose again so that everyone might live in the freedom of the Spirit. Barth contends that in Christ's "death there took place the regeneration and conversion of man."[5] The locus of our conversion is therefore an objective event, that which happened outside of us on the cross. Barth does make a place for conversion experiences, but in his theology these signify nothing but an awakening to the regeneration already effected by Jesus Christ.

Bultmann and the Christian existentialists take a quite different position. They maintain that the conversion of people to God takes place in the decision of faith as they hear the message of salvation (the kerygma). It is not the death on the cross so much as the proclamation of the cross that brings about conversion. Whereas Barth's position is objectivistic, existentialist theology is imperiled by subjectivism.

Those who stand in the tradition of evangelical revivalism equate conversion with the experience of the repentance of sins. It is the experience of the Spirit rather than a heroic decision of the will (as in existentialism) that is the main emphasis in Evangelicalism. This experience of the Spirit is never divorced from the decisive work on the cross, and this is the strength of the evangelical revivalist position. The danger lies in focusing our attention upon the experience rather than the object of the experience, namely, the crucified and risen Christ.

Roman Catholic theology and the older Lutheran theology point to sacramental baptism as the locus of conversion. It is in baptism, they maintain, even infant baptism, that people are regenerated or born anew by the Spirit. Although they acknowledge that the grace operative in baptism must bear fruit in repentance and faith, the necessity for personal faith is not given sufficient attention. Here it is possible to discern a sacramental objectivism.

---

[5] Karl Barth, *Church Dogmatics*, IV/2 (ed. G. W. Bromiley and T. F. Torrance), (Edinburgh: T. & T. Clark, 1958), p. 291.

In the older Reformed theology what is regarded as decisive for salvation is election to the covenant community. Since being born of Christian parents is one of the principal means by which a person is received into the covenant community, the emphasis is no longer upon individual conversion but upon belonging to the people of God. Reformed history has been marked by tension and even conflict between those who hold to the covenant idea and those who espouse a pietistic view of salvation. The New England Puritans who sought to include the children of believers in the covenant community nevertheless insisted upon personal faith as being essential for regeneration. John Cotton held that the blessings of the covenant extend to all children of believing parents; yet these blessings are effectually bestowed only upon those who enter into a living relationship with Christ.[6]

The new secular theology (Cox, J. A. T. Robinson, Van Buren, Howard Moody) speaks of commitment and involvement rather than conversion. The locus of this commitment is the present struggle for justice and equality. These theologians concentrate their attention on winning people over to the cause of social justice rather than a spiritual conversion to Christ.

Finally mention must be made of the debate over the scope of conversion — whether it concerns the social and political life of man as well as the spiritual. Pietism and Evangelicalism speak of the conversion of the inner man and the salvation of man's soul. Social reform is believed to be a consequence rather than the precondition of personal transformation. Religious socialists such as George MacLeod and secular theologians such as J. A. T. Robinson prefer to speak of the salvation of the whole man rather than the soul of man. These men insist that conversion must entail a change in one's social and economic attitudes as well as in one's relationship to God. The danger in the approach of secular theology is that the horizontal dimension of human existence is stressed to the detriment of the vertical dimension. One's relationship to God certainly determines and shapes one's relationship to his fellowman. At the same time a person whose heart is closed to the needs of his neighbor is not yet in a right relationship with God.

---

[6] Peter Y. DeJong, *The Covenant Idea in New England Theology* (Grand Rapids: Eerdmans, 1945), pp. 77-93.

CONVERSION AS EVENT AND PROCESS

I maintain that the locus of conversion is neither an outward religious rite nor an inward experience nor a past historical event but rather the Christian life.[7] Our conversion is certainly grounded in the objective work of God in Jesus Christ on Calvary, but it is misleading and even unbiblical to affirm that Christ was converted in our place. Jesus Christ did not need to be converted, since he was united with God at the very core of his being. But he chose to take upon himself the sin and guilt of the world so that sinners might be converted and gain life everlasting. Christ is the objective reality of our salvation, but this salvation must be appropriated in daily repentance under the cross. As Luther stated in the first of his ninety-five theses: "When our Lord and Master, Jesus Christ, said 'Repent,' He called for the entire life of believers to be one of repentance."

The drama of conversion can be said to unfold in various stages. The foundation of our conversion and renewal should be viewed as the cross of Calvary. The seed of conversion is given to us in the sacrament of Holy Baptism.[8] The realization and progression of conversion take place in the obedience of faith. Its consummation is glorification, life with Jesus Christ in eternity. Conversion begins in the action of the Spirit at baptism; it is fulfilled in the moment of decision. Or in the case of believers who are not baptized as infants, their conversion begins in the outreaching work of the Spirit through the gospel, and it is confirmed in sacramental baptism. Moreover, conversion continues throughout life as our relationship to God is deepened by the cleansing power of his Spirit. Conversion is therefore both an event and a process in that it entails an initial surrender to Jesus Christ as well as constant fidelity to him throughout life. It signifies both taking up the cross in the decision of faith and bearing the cross in a life of obedience.

The source and ground of our conversion is the free unmerited grace of God revealed and fulfilled in the death and resurrection of Jesus Christ. That God's decisive work of reconciliation in Christ is the pivotal center and foundation of our salvation must surely be

---

[7] See Donald G. Bloesch, *The Christian Life and Salvation* (Grand Rapids: Eerdmans, 1967).
[8] By the seed of conversion given in baptism I do not have in mind a spiritual or incorporeal substance, but rather the Holy Spirit who is now acting upon the child awakening within him the desire for salvation.

affirmed. As Blumhardt declared: "It is not so much the question whether a man suddenly decides to be converted. The first and most important thing is that God sets out to intervene for him and in the end wins him."[9]

Yet we must go on to affirm that God's grace must be appropriated by us if it is to be effectual for our salvation. The salvation procured by Jesus Christ must become a concrete reality in our lives. And this means that repentance or conversion is also decisive for our salvation. Calvin acknowledges that Christ "exposed himself to death, that he might redeem us from the sentence of death . . . but it is not enough for us unless we now receive him, that thus the efficacy and fruit of his death may reach us."[10] The victory that overcomes the world is not only the cross of Christ but also the faith of the believer (1 Jn 5:4).

The Protestant Reformers understood grace primarily as the favor or mercy of God rather than as a divine power or energy infused into man. Barth and Nygren also view grace in this way. Yet it must be said that grace in the biblical perspective is not only divine favor toward us but also creative divine power within us. Indeed, Christ not only dies for us, but he also lives within us by his Spirit, and only then is his salvation realized in our lives. For this reason we must affirm that there is no salvation apart from the mystical union between Christ and the believer which takes place in repentance and faith.

The relationship between grace and freedom can best be described in terms of paradox — divine grace operating in and through man's free decision. Paul gave cogent expression to this paradox of salvation: ". . . work out your own salvation with fear and trembling; for God is at work in you, both to will and to work for his good pleasure" (Phil. 2:12, 13). The paradox is that God effects man's salvation not apart from, but in and through, man's surrender and decision. Both God and man are active from the beginning to the end. Man is active, however, not on the basis of his natural freedom but on the basis of the freedom that comes to him from the Spirit. It is better therefore to speak of "the glorious liberty of the children of God" (Rom. 8:21) than free will. Man is by nature bound to the powers of sin and death, but he becomes free in

---

[9] R. Lejeune, ed., *Christoph Blumhardt and His Message*, pp. 97, 98.
[10] John Calvin, *Tracts and Treatises on the Doctrine and Worship of the Church* (trans. Henry Beveridge), (Grand Rapids: Eerdmans, 1958), II, p. 89.

the moment of decision when the Spirit empowers him to respond to the offer of the gospel. The paradox of salvation is that in the act of belief one is completely subjected to God and yet wholly free (Rom. 6).

This brings us to the relationship between conversion and regeneration. In the older Reformed theology regeneration signifies the work of God in the human heart, whereas conversion or repentance represents man's role in the drama of salvation. What is important to understand is that these two realities are not parallel processes but rather two ways of explaining the paradox of salvation. To affirm, as some revivalists have done, that we must give our hearts to Christ and then his Spirit will regenerate us, is to fall into a kind of semi-Pelagianism or synergism. The very fact that we do surrender our lives to Christ is a sign that regeneration by his Spirit is already taking place.

Conversion has been rightly associated with regeneration, since it entails not only a turning toward God but also an inward cleansing. It is well to bear in mind that sins are taken away in repentance and faith as well as forgiven. Christ saves us not only from the guilt and penalty of sin but also from its power. We are saved by Christ working within us through his Spirit as well as by Christ dying for us on the cross of Calvary.

Yet it is important to recognize that our regeneration, although beginning in a particular time, has still to be completed.[11] The work of renewal and purification is not accomplished all at once, but it must continue throughout the life of the Christian. Our carnal nature is crucified in baptism and faith but not yet eradicated. The new birth means that our life-orientation has been changed, not that our hearts have been completely purified. The Christian is still a sinner, even though he is on the way to being made righteous. In one sense he is no longer in sin because he is now united with Christ at the very core of his being. Yet vestiges of sin remain within him even though he is now rooted in the holiness of Christ. This is why our Reformed fathers spoke of the justification of the ungodly, which

---

[11] This indeed is the position of the Protestant Reformers, Calvin and Luther. It is interesting to note that Calvin includes sanctification under regeneration and thereby regards the latter as a process that extends throughout life. See François Wendel, *Calvin* (trans. Philip Mairet), (London: Collins, 1963), pp. 242-255. The Dutch theologian Hendrikus Berkhof treats both justification and sanctification as elements within regeneration. See his *The Doctrine of the Holy Spirit* (Richmond, Va.: John Knox, 1964), pp. 68-75.

means that believers despite their sin are justified. At the same time, we need also to speak of the justification of the converted, since it is only those who believe that are declared to be righteous in Christ.

Regeneration like conversion can be regarded as both an event and a process in that the Holy Spirit seeks to consummate what he has begun. We err both by viewing the initiatory stage of regeneration as the climax of the Spirit's work and by treating regeneration as a general life process that entails no decisive break with the past. Regeneration in the broad sense involves the whole work of cleansing and renovation, but in a narrower sense it can be regarded as the act or acts by which one is received into communion with Christ. Even in this more limited sense regeneration can be held to occur in a series of stages beginning with the seeking for Christ by the prompting of his Spirit and ending in commitment to Christ in the power of his Spirit.

Regeneration is closely associated with sanctification and may be said even to include it. Both terms refer to different aspects of the same process, but it is possible to make a formal distinction between them. Regeneration can be understood as participation in Christ, being engrafted into Christ, while sanctification connotes obedience and conformity to Christ in life and work.[12] Whereas regeneration means entering upon a new existence, sanctification is concerned with the development of a holy personality. Regeneration signifies the washing away of sin and inward spiritual renewal; sanctification means being set apart from the world for consecrated service (cf. Eph. 5:26, 27). We must not only receive the Spirit in faith but also be directed by the Spirit in love to follow the path of our Master. Our participation in the revivifying power of Jesus Christ begins in the crisis of repentance and faith; we are turned in an altogether new direction, but we are not yet made whole. The cleansing and renewing work of the Spirit must continue until we are wholly conformed to his image. Consequently we are not fully regenerate until we are entirely sanctified. It can be said that sanctification has its commencement in regeneration and that regeneration finds its fulfillment in sanctification.

---

[12] It should be noted that our engrafting into Christ is a process as well as an event. Even though we may now be members of the mystical body of Christ, we constantly need to be engrafted ever more fully into this body.

Justification is our acceptance by God and is indeed the ground of our regeneration and sanctification. Justification occurs simultaneously with regeneration in that we receive God's grace only by participation in Christ through faith. Yet in contradistinction to both the dominant strand of Roman Catholic theology and Schleiermacher, I affirm that the cause of justification is not our inner renewal but rather the free grace or mercy of God.

LIFELONG CONVERSION

Because Christians are still sinners, even they need to be converted In the New Testament believers are called upon to repent and turn again to Christ (cf. Lk. 17:3, 4; 22:32; Rev. 2:5, 16, 21; 3:19). It is Christians who are urged to be renewed in mind and spirit and to put on the new nature (Eph. 4:22-24; Rom. 13:14). In Ezekiel the call to repentance is addressed to the house of Israel (Ezek. 14:6. 18:30, 31; cf. 1 Kings 8:46-50). The psalmist was moved to pray "Create in me a clean heart, O God, and put a new and right spirit within me" (Ps. 51:10). Surely this prayer should also be found on the lips of Christians. Johann Arndt has declared: "We are to be daily renewed through Christ and His Holy Gospel, daily reborn by God's Word, becoming new selves."[13] This is not to imply that the Christian is always in and out of the kingdom as if he were caught in a revolving door; rather once having entered he needs to remain true to his calling and constantly to renew his commitment to Christ. We should perhaps say that the Christian stands in need not so much of reconversion as of deeper conversion. We are incorporated into Christ in the decision of faith, but we have not yet been brought into perfect obedience to Christ. The difference between the Christian and the non-Christian is that the former is a forgiven sinner, a sinner who has already been turned to the pathway of sacrificial love although he is not yet perfected in love.

Moreover, we are told that we can fall out of our conversion (cf Ezek. 18:24; Gal. 5:4; Heb. 4:6; 6:4-6; 1 Tim. 1:19; 2 Pet. 2:20, 21). It is not enough to have made a decision for Christ; we must persevere in this decision. We can have certainty of our salvation in that Christ promises his grace to all who call upon him in faith, but

---

[13] Johann Arndt, *Devotions and Prayers of Johann Arndt* (ed. & trans. John Joseph Stoudt), (Grand Rapids: Baker, 1958), p. 8.

we do not have that kind of security whereby we can rest content and cease striving for the crown of eternal life. Paul warned: "Therefore let any one who thinks that he stands take heed lest he fall" (1 Cor. 10:12). John Bunyan also discerned the precarious nature of the Christian pilgrimage: "Then I saw that there was a way to hell, even from the gates of heaven."[14] Calvin, despite his doctrines of predestination and perseverance, could affirm that "the moment we turn away even slightly from him, our salvation, which rests firmly in him, gradually vanishes away."[15] To be sure, Calvin would assert that only those who continually rest in Christ are truly elected by God.

It must be recognized that the only mortal sin is unbelief. It is only this sin that completely sunders the mystical bond between the Christian and his God. Other sins that grow out of unbelief simply confirm the wretchedness of our state and serve also to keep us out of the kingdom (Rev. 21:8). But it is unbelief in particular that the writer of Hebrews has in mind when he affirms that there can be no second repentance for the fallen away sinner (6:4-6). Indeed, is not this the sin against the Holy Spirit, to refuse the grace and mercy of God and choose to walk by one's own light (cf. Is. 50:11; Lk. 12:10)? At the same time there is the outside possibility that a sinner fallen away may be reclaimed by the grace of God and regenerated anew (cf. Jer. 30:17; Rom. 11:23).

The Holiness-Pentecostal movement has rightly discerned that the experience of conversion is not sufficient for full salvation, and that we must seek to go on to perfection (Heb. 6:1). These Christians contend that conversion must be supplemented by the experience of sanctification (also called the second blessing, entire sanctification, Christian perfection, or the baptism of the Holy Spirit). I maintain that conversion begins with the baptism of the Spirit and that it is continued and carried forward by an abiding in the Spirit. Entire or perfect sanctification can be approximated in this life, but it cannot be truly attained until death and the hereafter. This is not to deny that there might very well be deeper experiences of the Spirit subsequent to conversion, special anointings that equip Christians for service to their Master in the world. But we must be

---

[14] John Bunyan, *The Pilgrim's Progress* (Philadelphia: John C. Winston, 1933), I, XI, p. 169.
[15] Calvin, *Institutes* (McNeill ed.), II, 16, 1, p. 503.

on guard against equating such experiences with a state of perfection and also viewing any particular charisma or gift as the evidential sign of having the Spirit.

In my view, the Christian life is characterized not so much by climactic experiences as by daily repentance and obedience under the cross. It is not the experience of conversion as such but perseverance in conversion that is decisive for salvation. We need not only to receive the salvation of Christ but also to continue in this salvation if the crown of glory is finally to be ours. Adolf Köberle has rightly said that "daily renewal, the daily journey to the Cross is extolled by Scripture as the only possible expression of a living state of faith and that it holds good even for the one who has been justified."[16]

It is well to bear in mind that the Christian life is also a victorious life. The Spirit of Christ empowers us for combat against the forces of darkness in the world. Through the Spirit we can conquer every foe and truly ascend toward the summit of the perfection to which Christ calls us. That the Christian can make real progress in holiness is testified to by Paul: "And we all . . . beholding the glory of the Lord, are being changed into his likeness from one degree of glory to another" (2 Cor. 3:18). The Christian cannot arrive at the goal of perfection in love in this life, but he or she can attain a spiritual maturity that mirrors and proclaims the perfect holiness of Jesus Christ.

It should be said that the degree of our progress by no means determines our standing in the sight of God, since our justification is to be attributed to faith alone. We are able to proceed toward holiness because we are justified; justification is not imputed to us on the basis of our holiness. On the other hand, if we cease to make progress and begin to fall away from faith, our standing before God will be imperiled.

THE FRUITS AND MEANS OF CONVERSION

Conversion itself is not accessible to psychological analysis, since it consists in the regeneration of the heart by the Spirit of God. But its fruits are certainly discernible to the eye of natural man. Indeed, Jesus said that by their fruits will you know them (Mt. 7:16, 20).

---

[16] Adolf Köberle, *The Quest for Holiness* (Minneapolis: Augsburg, 1938), p. 224.

Empirical piety is not the basis of conversion, but it is a confirmatory sign of our conversion.

What are some of the fruits of conversion? Certainly joy must be mentioned. C. S. Lewis speaks of being "surprised by joy" in coming to know the salvation of Christ.[17] Self-control, peace, patience, and kindness are also fruits of the Spirit (Gal. 5:22, 23). But surely love is the highest of the fruits, the crown of the virtues (1 Cor. 13), and apart from love the other virtues are to no avail. In Galatians 5:22 Paul gives precedence to love, and we can surmise that the other fruits he mentions are none other than the fruit of love. Indeed love contains within itself all the other virtues (1 Cor. 13), binding them together in perfect harmony (Col. 3:14).

One significant fruit and sign of conversion that should not be overlooked is humility. In the words of Isaiah: "But this is the man to whom I will look, he that is humble and contrite in spirit, and trembles at my word" (66:2). Paul warns us against self-conceit (Gal. 5:26). Peter urges us to clothe ourselves with humility (1 Pet. 5:5). We should be humble because even after conversion we remain finite creatures and sinners. Humility is born out of contrition, and contrition rests upon the consciousness of sin. It was this insight that impelled Kierkegaard to write: "The consciousness of sin is the 'conditio sine qua non' of Christianity."[18] This is why the Christian life consists in daily humiliation as well as in increasing victory over sin.

Concerning the means of conversion evangelical theology gives primary attention to the preaching and hearing of the Word of God. It is mainly by the gospel proclamation that people are convicted of sin and come to a saving knowledge of Christ (cf. Rom. 10:14-17; 1 Cor. 1:21; 2 Cor. 5:20). The sacraments, such as baptism and the Lord's Supper, are viewed as secondary means of grace. They are considered means of grace only in association with the Word. But this is not to underestimate their significance in the plan of salvation. Baptism sets us on the way; Holy Communion keeps us on the way. Neither rite has efficacy apart from faith, since faith alone is indispensable for salvation. Yet grace is objectively present in the sacraments apart from faith, even in infant baptism. This grace

---

[17] See C. S. Lewis, *Surprised by Joy* (New York: Harcourt, Brace and World, 1966).
[18] Søren Kierkegaard, *The Journals of Søren Kierkegaard* (ed. & trans. Alexander Dru), (London: Oxford University Press, 1951), p. 131.

does not benefit us concretely, however, unless it is fulfilled in repentance and faith.

This brings us to the question of whether the Christian life itself can be viewed as a means of conversion. The Christian life is in one sense a fruit of conversion, but does not it also contribute to our conversion? The secular theologians speak of "Christian presence" as being the key to evangelism and see this as a substitute for evangelical preaching. Christian presence simply means being with and for people in the world, identifying oneself with them rather than preaching at them. This position has some merit, but can we really reach people for the gospel without telling them about it?

In my view the Christian life, like the sacraments, can be regarded as a secondary means of grace so long as it is accompanied by and proceeds from the proclamation of the Word of God. The life of faithful obedience will not only strengthen the man of faith in his conversion, but it will also be instrumental in the conversion of unbelievers. Jesus tells his disciples: "Let your light so shine before men, that they may see your good works and give glory to your Father who is in heaven" (Mt. 5:16; cf. 1 Pet. 2:12). Paul says that by his word *and deed* Gentiles were won to Christian obedience (Rom. 15:18). He declares to the Corinthians: "You yourselves are our letter of recommendation, written on your hearts, to be known and read by all men; and you show that you are a letter from Christ delivered by us . . ." (2 Cor. 3:2, 3). Peter contends that husbands may be won to Christ simply by the behavior of their wives (1 Pet. 3:1). The fruits of conversion are also means of conversion, but this does not take away from the decisive role of preaching of the Word. Indeed, to speak the truth of the Word of God in love can be considered the prime fruit of conversion, and this is also the prime means of grace. Word and life belong together, and unless both are present conversion cannot really take place.

CONVERSION AND SOCIAL REFORM

This brings us to the third major area of debate concerning conversion, namely, its relationship to social reform. As has been said, on the one hand are those who contend that conversion refers primarily to man's relationship to God, and the change in his social attitudes is a result of a previous spiritual change. On the other hand, we have those who maintain that conversion is an event that encompasses the whole of man's life and that the change in his social attitudes is an integral part of conversion itself.

My position is that conversion is basically a change in one's relationship to God but that this spiritual change entails a transformation in social attitudes as well. Conversion is primarily a spiritual event, but it has profound implications in the secular or public sphere of our lives. It points us toward a spiritual goal, but we are called to pursue this spiritual goal in the midst of the grime and agony of the world.

This is not to imply that social righteousness is an automatic consequence of individual regeneration. It is simply not true, as popular piety sometimes expresses it, that when everyone becomes a Christian, we shall then have a Christian society. This would be the case if conversion entailed perfection, but the newly converted Christian is far from perfect. Indeed, because sin persists within the Christian even unto his death, he needs to be disciplined and restrained by law just as the non-Christian. A significant difference is that the genuinely converted believer recognizes his frailty and deficiency and thereby is able to resist the temptation to idolatry. It must also be said that the Christian is able to bring the spirit of Agape love into the political arena and can therefore be much more sensitive than the nonbeliever to the dire needs of humanity. The temptation of those who stand in the tradition of evangelicalism is to claim too much for conversion.[19] But the peril in the circles of neo-liberalism and neo-orthodoxy is to fail to recognize that conversion entails an ontological change, that the converted person is now a "new creation" (2 Cor. 5:17).

I cannot subscribe to the belief rampant among the devotees of the older Lutheran orthodoxy that the Christian lives in two separate spheres, the spiritual and the secular. The truth in this position is that the spiritual and the secular do signify two different

---

[19] This error can also be seen in Schleiermacher, who adhered to the older Pietist concept that man is restored to wholeness in regeneration; thereby he was unable to do justice to the truth that the Christian is still a real sinner. He declared: "Sin in the new man is no longer active; it is only the after-effect of the old man. The new man thus no longer takes sin to be his own; he indeed labours against it as something foreign to him. The consciousness of guilt is thus abolished." In his *The Christian Faith* (eds. H. R. Mackintosh and J. S. Stewart), (New York: Harper & Row, 1963), II, p. 498.

dimensions, but they must not be separated. When Jesus said that we should give unto Caesar the things that are Caesar's and unto God the things that are God's (Mt. 22:21), he was not implying that life is divided between Caesar's rule and God's but that all of life belongs to God; the little that belongs to Caesar by God's permission can be returned to Caesar. In the view of Jesus, even Pilate derives his authority and power from God (Jn. 19:11). The secular state is not a kingdom that can demand absolute allegiance but rather a political society brought into being for the purpose of maintaining law and order. Moreover, it is in such a society that we are called to work out our vocation to Christian sainthood.

The Bible does, however, speak of an invisible spiritual kingdom that is opposed to the rule of God and has entered into the world corrupting the loyalties of individuals and nations. It is this kingdom, the kingdom of darkness, that we are called to battle in the name of Christ. But this battle takes place on every level of human life, including the political and economic spheres as well as the spiritual. When the state becomes enslaved to the powers of darkness, when it demands for itself unconditional loyalty, then Christians must protest, and they must make this protest known in every area of life. When the state pretends to be a kingdom that encompasses all of life, a self-sustaining political order, a power unto itself, then Christians must be prepared to "obey God rather than men" (Acts 5:29).

The converted sinner will be primarily concerned about the spiritual lostness of man, but he will also agonize over the injustices that the lost condition of man engenders. The church as a church should generally beware of getting involved in partisan politics because its mission is fundamentally spiritual. It is called to herald a gospel concerning a kingdom that is not of this world. It is commissioned to prepare people for membership in a heavenly, not a secular, city. At the same time, when political issues become moral issues, then the church must speak to the political situation. When the life and work of our fellowmen are placed in jeopardy, the church dare not remain silent. But what it speaks must be the Word of God and not a political or sociological opinion.

We must be careful not to identify the gospel with a social crusade or a program for social reform. This does not mean that we as Christians should not take part in movements that seek to bring about social reform, such as the civil rights movement. On the contrary, wherever people are seeking a just social order we should lend them our earnest support. Indeed, Christians should be in the vanguard of those who seek to correct the inequities and injustices within society. Yet we must always remember that social reform does not of itself prepare the way for the kingdom of God. Nor is a relatively just society in this world ever to be equated with the holy city of the saints prophesied in the New Testament (cf. Heb. 11:10, 16; 13:14; Rev. 21:2, 10). We must also bear in mind that evangelizing is not the same thing as humanizing or civilizing, as Bishop Robinson has contended.[20] Nor is evangelism to be equated with social action as in the writings of Harvey Cox and Colin Williams.

It is becoming commonplace to affirm that Christianity has destroyed the demarcation between sacred and secular. The danger of this position is that it leads one to view the mission of the church solely as social service and conversion as a purely psychological change that facilitates integration with one's social environment. But conversion signifies in the first instance not a new social attitude nor a richer personal life nor a new self-understanding but rather a spiritual rebirth, a new existence, which is a gift of the Spirit of God. This new birth will have repercussions in every area of a person's life and may very well lead to social concern and psychological integration. But the trouble today is that we are putting the cart before the horse and seeking to change the environment without changing the person. Kierkegaard had some wise words for us on this point: "Oh, let us never forget this, let us not reduce the spiritual to the worldly. Even though we may earnestly think of the spiritual and the worldly together, let us forever distinguish between them."[21]

The truth in the position of those who uphold a secular theology is that man needs bread as well as the Bread of Life. He has need of freedom and equality of opportunity as well as the freedom of the Spirit. He rightly yearns for freedom from oppression and slavery as well as for freedom from sin. Yet we must forever hold on to the biblical truth that man does not live by bread alone (Lk. 4:4). The

---

[20] See J. A. T. Robinson, *On Being the Church in the World* (London: SCM, 1960), p. 19.

[21] Søren Kierkegaard, *Purity of Heart* (trans. Douglas Steere), (New York: Harper, 1956), p. 181.

one thing needful is the hearing of the Word of God (Lk. 10:42). That which is indispensable for the abundant life that Christ came to give us is conversion by the power of his Spirit.

Seven

TWO TYPES OF SPIRITUALITY

THE TWO TYPES DEFINED

IN THE HISTORY of the Christian church two basic types of spirituality can be discerned, the mystical and the evangelical. These are ideal types, to be sure, and are only partially exemplified in the various theological systems and devotional writings. Yet this typology is helpful for understanding the concerns that grip theologians and the vision that governs their thought. Mystical spirituality has been dominant in Roman Catholicism and Eastern Orthodoxy, whereas evangelical devotion characterizes the mainstream of Protestantism. This is not to deny, however, that many Protestants have also been mystics and some of the Catholic saints have been strongly evangelical and biblical as well.

Mystical spirituality, as we find in Christendom, has two principal sources, the Bible and Neo-Platonism. The syncretistic mystery religions of the ancient Graeco-Roman world also played a role in the development of Christian mysticism. In the writings of the great mystics one can detect a tension between biblical piety and Hellenistic philosophy. In more recent times, since the Enlightenment, mystical piety in the Christian world has appropriated insights from Hinduism and Buddhism. Particularly in Protestant transcendentalist groups (such as New Thought and Unity), the biblical roots of mysticism are obscured by a syncretistic religion in which Oriental philosophical thought is very prominent.

81

Among the great mystics of the Eastern Church were Dionysius, John of Damascus, Gregory of Nyssa, and Basil the Great. In the medieval church there were Augustine, Thomas Aquinas, Meister Eckhart, Jan van Ruysbroeck, Henry Suso, Catherine of Genoa, Catherine of Sienna, Richard Rolle, Thomas à Kempis, and Johann Tauler. Post-medieval or modern Roman Catholic mystics are Teresa of Avila, John of the Cross, Brother Lawrence, Fénelon, Garrigou-Lagrange, and Thomas Merton. Noted Protestant mystics are Jacob Boehme, William Law, Gerhard Tersteegen, and Johann Arndt. In more recent times we might list Gerald Heard, Albert Day, the Quaker mystics Rufus Jones and Douglas Steere, Evelyn Underhill, and probably also Friedrich Schleiermacher and Paul Tillich.

Evangelical devotion is wholly biblical, being grounded in the Old Testament as well as the New. This kind of spirituality has also been called biblical personalism (E. Brunner) in order to distinguish it from a monistic mystical religion in which personality is negated or transcended. Its hallmark is the doctrine of justification by free grace, which stands in contradistinction to the way of works-righteousness that characterizes nearly all world religions. Here we can mention the prophets such as Isaiah and Jeremiah, the Gospel writers, St. Paul, Irenaeus, the Reformers Luther and Calvin, Richard Baxter, John Bunyan, John Wesley, and Jonathan Edwards. In the modern and contemporary periods we can point to Kierkegaard, General William Booth, Christoph Blumhardt, Dwight L. Moody, Karl Heim, P. T. Forsyth, Reinhold Niebuhr, Emil Brunner, Dietrich Bonhoeffer, Karl Barth, and G. C. Berkouwer. The ecumenical Roman Catholic theologian Hans Küng might also be mentioned, inasmuch as his theology, at least in its earlier phase, was oriented about the biblical message of justification by divine grace. Moreover, he draws sharp lines of distinction between biblical faith and mysticism.[1]

It must be recognized that there are many thinkers and devotional writers through the ages who have sought to combine mystical and evangelical piety. Such a synthesis can already be seen in John and even in Paul. Catholic writers who have at least one foot in evangelicalism are Augustine, Thomas Aquinas, Bernard of

---

[1] See Hans Küng, *Freedom Today* (trans. Cecily Hastings), (New York: Sheed and Ward, 1966), pp. 136, 137, 147.

Clairvaux, Johann Tauler, Thomas à Kempis, John of the Cross, and Pascal. We should also mention in more recent times Hugo and Karl Rahner, Thomas Merton, and Thérèse of Lisieux, who spoke of a lift to heaven in contrast to the ladder of merit. Among Protestants who have sought to appropriate what is biblically valid in mystical spirituality are the early Luther, Calvin, the Pietists Philip Jacob Spener and August Francke, George Fox, Richard Baxter, Jonathan Edwards, and Holiness devotional writers such as Andrew Murray, Hannah W. Smith, and Agnes Sanford. The more authentic Protestant mystics, Johann Arndt and Gerhard Tersteegen, also are evangelical in much of their orientation. Such guiding lights of the religious community movement in modern Protestantism as Mother Basilea Schlink, founder of the Ecumenical Sisterhood of Mary, and Max Thurian of the Community of Taizé, also mirror both types of spirituality. It should be said that there is a mystical element in all evangelical religion just as there must be an evangelical element in any mysticism that would call itself Christian.

Two noted historians of religion, Friedrich Heiler, a convert from Catholicism to Lutheranism, and Nathan Söderblom, have sought to do justice to the perennially valid insights in both kinds of spirituality. At the same time, they both definitely lean toward the evangelical side, inasmuch as the biblical message of free grace is their basic criterion. Söderblom distinguishes between "the mysticism of personal life," which has biblical foundation, and the "mysticism of the infinite," which signifies monistic pantheism. Heiler in his famous book *Prayer* draws a distinction between prophetic religion, which is more inclusive than evangelical biblical faith, and mystical religion. He maintains with some cogency that authentic mysticism sharply contradicts the main thrust of biblical religion.[2]

MYSTICAL SPIRITUALITY

In determining the nature of mystical religion we must first bear in mind that our concern is with the kind of mysticism that has penetrated into the life of the Christian church. Inasmuch as all mysticism is oriented about spiritual experience, there will be

---

[2] See Friedrich Heiler, *Prayer* (trans. Samuel McComb), (New York: Oxford University Press, 1958).

much in common between Christian and pagan mysticism. At the same time, since the Christian is committed to the incarnation of God in Jesus Christ, Christian mysticism will reflect biblical motifs as well.

The first earmark of mystical religion is that it is centered in direct or immediate experience of ultimate reality. This experience is described by Augustine: "with the flash of a trembling glance," his mind "arrived at that which is."[3] Christian mystics have commonly identified this reality with Jesus Christ or the Word of God, but they have also envisaged it in more impersonal terms, such as the World Spirit, the infinite, and the ground of being. Catherine of Genoa seldom referred to Christ in her writings and spoke primarily of the experience of God.

A second characteristic of mysticism is that this experience is regarded as an encounter with mystery and thereby as ineffable. The mystical experience, one interpreter says, "entirely transcends our sensory-intellectual consciousness."[4] According to the author of *The Cloud of Unknowing*, intellectually the soul is blank in contemplation.[5] The mystic will often write about his experience but always differentiating his description from the thing itself. Many of the great mystics have been content to describe their experience in negative terms, i.e., to explain what it is not.

This brings us to the conception of God in mystical religion. All the mystics, both Christian and pagan, seek to overcome what they consider to be the anthropomorphic understanding of God. The Christian mystics often refer to God as "Father" and sometimes as "Everlasting King," but they insist that these terms are to be understood only symbolically. The Neo-Platonic philosopher Plotinus identified God with "the One" that transcends all existence. In mystical literature God is often depicted as being above and beyond being (Gregory of Nyssa, Origen, Eckhart). He is the source and ground of all existence. He is both the World Soul and the core and center of the human soul. He is frequently spoken of as "the undifferentiated unity." He is "above love and affection" (Meister Eckhart). We "cannot even say . . . that he is an objective

---

[3] Augustine, *Confessions* vii. 17. In Whitney J. Oates, ed., *Basic Writings of Saint Augustine* (New York: Random House, 1948), I, p. 105.
[4] Walter T. Stace, *The Teachings of the Mystics* (New York: Mentor, 1960), p. 15.
[5] Clifton Wolters, ed., *The Cloud of Unknowing* (Baltimore: Penguin, 1961), pp. 53ff.

reality" (Berdyaev).[6] A distinction is sometimes made between God and the Godhead (Eckhart, Ruysbroeck) or between God in his self-manifestation and God in his abysmal nature (Tillich), thereby allowing for the participation of God in human existence. To come to God means to descend into the soul, to journey to the center. The image of God in man is interpreted in terms of a divine spark implanted in the human heart. In mystical religion and philosophy man is understood as being in basic continuity with God.

Faith for the mystics is an ecstatic state of being grasped by mystery (Tillich). It consists in a transcending of the subject-object cleavage. It is a participation in God or the ultimate reality rather than a confrontation by this reality. The "dark night of faith" refers to the soul's being overwhelmed or blinded by the uncreated light of God (John of the Cross).

Grace in the Christian mystical tradition is generally envisaged as an infused power by which our nature is transformed or divinized. The early church fathers often spoke of the divinization and deification of man by grace. Athanasius said that Christ became man so that man might become God.[7] The late medieval mystic Catherine of Genoa went so far as to affirm: "My being is God, not by simple participation but by a true transformation of my being."[8]

The mystical concept of grace is closely bound up with that of merit by which man is made worthy of the glory of God. Mystics are invariably ascetics, since they must seek to prepare themselves by rigorous discipline for the privileges of divine sonship. Yet they generally state that their merits are none other than gifts of God. Moreover, the possibility of self-salvation is denied in the mainstream of Christian mysticism at the last stage of union. As Tillich reminds us: "In spite of all the preparations, the ecstatic reunion with the ultimate cannot be forced when this point has been reached. It must be given, yet might not be given at all."[9]

---

[6] Nicolas Berdyaev, *Truth and Revelation* (trans. R. M. French), (New York: Collier, 1962), p. 112.

[7] Athanasius, *The Incarnation of the Word of God* (introduction by C. S. Lewis), (New York: Macmillan, 1946), p. 93.

[8] Quoted in Evelyn Underhill, *The Mystics of the Church* (New York: Schocken, 1964), p. 165.

[9] Paul Tillich, *Systematic Theology* (University of Chicago, 1957), II, p. 83. A mystic such as Eckhart could declare that God acts "purely because of his simple goodness and mercy. . . . Our works serve in no way to induce God to give to us or to do

The authority for the mystic is none other than the spiritual or mystical experience. Quaker mystics have often called this "the inner light." Schleiermacher spoke of the "feeling of absolute dependence" on God. Some mystics who are more biblically oriented refer to the new birth or the baptism of the Spirit. Yet it must be recognized that for most mystics the basis of authority is subjective. In the words of one interpreter: "For the mystic, whatever his professed creed, final authority lies in his own experience."[10]

In mystical religion love is understood primarily as "Eros," the seeking of self-fulfillment and self-transcendence. "Eros" is defined by Nygren as egocentric and acquisitive love.[11] Plato in his *Symposium* spoke of the ladder of love by which man raises himself to the heavenly realm. In medieval Catholic piety this ladder of love became a ladder of merit by which people sought to work their way into heaven with the aid of infused grace. Many Christian mystics have sought to reconcile the mystical ladder with Jacob's ladder, which pictured God descending as well as man ascending. In genuinely Catholic spirituality it is on the basis of God's grace to man that man is able to ascend to God. The medieval *caritas* signifies the synthesis of Eros and Agape — it is both a gift of God and the sum of all virtues (Nygren).

The ascent of the soul to God is often pictured in mystical writings in terms of three stages — purgation, illumination, and union. This schema actually comes from Dionysius, who in turn appropriated it from the Neo-Platonic philosopher Proclus. These stages are in turn divided into substages. The highest stage within union is called by some mystical writers "spiritual marriage," in which the soul is completely transfigured and upon death goes directly into heaven (without the intermediate state of purgatory). Such a soul is pictured as being totally sanctified or perfected. The final goal is the beatific vision of God, which is generally believed to occur only after death. It is interesting to note that the actual term comes from Plato, although the New Testament speaks of beholding the glory of God (Jn. 17:24; 2 Cor. 3:18). Having attained the ultimate goal, one enjoys a state of beatitude and ineffable peace.

---

anything." Quoted in Rudolf Otto, *Mysticism East and West* (trans. Bertha Bracey and Richenda Payne), (New York: Meridian, 1960), p. 129.

[10] Sidney Spencer, *Mysticism in World Religion* (Baltimore: Penguin, 1963), p. 337.
[11] Anders Nygren, *Agape and Eros* (trans. Philip Watson), (Philadelphia: Westminster, 1953), pp. 175-181.

The soul is not annihilated but rather wholly possessed by God. In the mainstream of Christian mysticism it is believed that only by divine grace can one attain the vision of God, although one can prepare the way for this dispensation by ascetic spiritual exercises.

Prayer is interpreted in mystical circles as meditation and contemplation rather than supplication. Aldous Huxley, who is to be counted among the syncretists, has declared: ". . . the practical teaching of Indian and Christian mystics is identical in such matters as . . . renunciation of petitionary prayer in favour of simple abandonment to the will of God."[12] In Roman Catholic theology petitionary prayer is accepted, but as a first step on the way to mystical prayer or contemplation. The Protestant mystic Johann Arndt distinguished between verbal prayer, inner prayer, and transcendent prayer, regarding the last, which is practically equivalent to contemplation, as the highest form of prayer. Because God is envisaged as a transpersonal ground of being, petitionary prayer must invariably give way to contemplative adoration.

Closely related to the mystical conception of prayer is the mystic stress on solitude and detachment from the things of the world. Plotinus describes the way of mysticism as "the flight of the alone to the alone." John of Damascus calls solitude "the mother of prayer." Whitehead, who stands in the tradition of Platonic mysticism, has stated: "Religion is what the individual does with his solitariness."[13] John Climacus defined prayer as "estrangement from the world, both visible and invisible."[14] The advice of Thomas à Kempis was: "Seek out a place apart, and love the solitary life. Do not engage in conversation with men. . . . Remain detached from acquaintances and friends and independent of this world's consolations."[15] Meister Eckhart went so far as to maintain that seclusion and disinterestedness are preferable to love. In mystical circles the need for detachment and separation from the creaturely is spoken of as "the call to the desert." This is to be understood metaphorically,

---

[12] Christopher Isherwood, ed., *Vedanta for the Western World* (New York: Viking, 1960), p. 105.
[13] Alfred North Whitehead, *Religion In the Making* (New York: Macmillan, 1926), p. 47.
[14] Quoted in Hilda Graef, *The Story of Mysticism* (New York: Doubleday, 1965), p. 127.
[15] Thomas à Kempis, *The Imitation of Christ* (trans. Leo Sherley-Price), (Baltimore: Penguin, 1959), p. 164.

since the "desert" signifies the absence of sensory and experiential supports. John of the Cross described it as the dark night of faith. Some mystics speak of a journey to the center, to the ground or core of the soul. The orientation in mysticism is predominately intro-spective, away from the exterior world into the interior world.[16] Eckhart put it this way: "When a person turns from temporal things inwards, into himself, he becomes aware of a heavenly light that does come from heaven."[17] And in Schleiermacher's words: ". . . as often as I turn my gaze inward upon my inmost self, I am at once within the domain of eternity."[18]

The emphasis upon detachment and separation from the crea-turely accounts for the glorification of celibacy in mystical religion and the disparagement of marriage. Some mystics, such as Nicolaus of Flue, left their wives and children in order to cultivate the interior life of devotion. Angela of Folino even prayed for the death of her family so that she might be free to give her life wholly to God. John Cassian said that it is impossible for married people to reach the heights of contemplation. Thomas Aquinas regarded the mar-ried state as sanctioned and blessed by God, but at the same time he held that the way of celibacy and poverty is a surer road to the kingdom of heaven.

It should be said that a biblical, evangelical note can be detected among many Christian mystics, in their stress upon the need for service to the poor and unfortunates. In their view the contempla-tive life is higher than the active life but it should always be related to and give rise to action in the world. The ultimate goal in life is union with God, but works of love as well as mystical prayer are the road to this union. Eckhart said that if one were in rapture and a sick man needed help, it would be better to come out of the rapture and show love by serving the man in need. Catherine of Genoa was the founder of the first hospital in Genoa and spent most of her life caring for the sick. Catherine of Sienna was immersed in the political life of her time and was instrumental in moving the papacy from Avignon back to Rome. Thomas Merton maintains that

---

[16] Rudolf Otto draws a distinction between the "mysticism of introspection" and the "mysticism of unifying vision," but he holds that the two types are intermingled in most mystical systems. See his *Mysticism East and West*, pp. 38-53.

[17] Raymond B. Blakney, ed., *Meister Eckhart* (New York: Harper, 1941), p. 192.

[18] Friedrich Schleiermacher, *Schleiermacher's Soliloquies* (trans. Horace L. Friess), (Chicago: Open Court, 1957), p. 22

contemplation is fulfilled in loving service: "The highest vocation in the Kingdom of God is that of sharing one's contemplation with others and bringing other men to the experimental knowledge of God that is given to those who love him perfectly."[19] Mother Catherine Thomas, a Carmelite nun, points to gratefulness as the motivation for service: "When I thought of what my Beloved had done for me I could not logically shrink from attempting to suffer something for Him, to spend myself, wear myself out, to return in some measure His gift."[20]

In mystical piety Jesus is generally upheld as the perfect revelation or mirror of divine love rather than as a substitutionary sacrifice for sin. He reveals and exemplifies the essential unity between God and man. He is sometimes spoken of as the Representative Man (William Law), the exemplar of perfected human nature (Schleiermacher), the Quickener of the higher self-consciousness (Schleiermacher), and the Elder Brother (Gerald Heard). Occasionally he is viewed as the first emergence of a new order of beings, the New Adam. Some of the mystics who are closer to the mainstream of Christian tradition affirm the hypostatic union of the two natures in Christ, but even in their writings it is the perfect obedience of Jesus rather than God's reconciling action in Christ that is made the focal point of attention. Jesus is upheld as our example, the model of perfect sainthood. Consequently among the Christian mystics we find a marked emphasis upon the *imitatio Christi* (the imitation of Christ). By his suffering and death Jesus shows the way to perfection. Many mystics see themselves as saviors with Christ, since they too seek to bear the cross of vicarious suffering and thereby attain union with the divine. In the purer forms of mysticism the picture of the humanity of Jesus is regarded as only a preparation for contemplation, and in the higher stages of mystical life the devout soul seeks to divest himself of all sensible images. The mystic way is to proceed beyond the human and historical Christ to the vision of the Highest Good. Augustine's axiom that "through the man Christ you reach the God Christ" accurately describes the dominant motif of Christian mysticism.

---

[19] Thomas Merton, *Seeds of Contemplation* (Norfolk, Conn.: James Laughlin, 1949), p. 185.
[20] Catherine Thomas, *My Beloved* (New York: McGraw-Hill, 1955), p. 134.

EVANGELICAL DEVOTION

Whereas mysticism places the accent upon the immanence of God, the evangelical tradition upholds the transcendence and majesty of God. The Christian mystics verge toward a monistic understanding of reality, while the evangelicals are dualistic in orientation. Kierkegaard echoes the prophetic strand in biblical religion when he speaks of "an infinite qualitative difference" between God and man.[21] God is other than man not only because he is the heavenly Creator and man is the finite creature, but also because he is holy and man is a sinner. Some of the mystics also speak of God as "the Wholly Other," but by this they usually mean that he transcends the compass of human cognition. For them God is the Wholly Other in an epistemological but not in an ontological nor a moral sense.

Moreover in prophetic religion God is envisaged as a personal being rather than an impersonal ground of being. God infinitely transcends human personality, but this does not mean that he is beyond personality; rather he is divine personality. God is not an anthropomorphic being, a "man upstairs," as we find this expressed in primitive religion; rather he is the infinite being who is the ground and source of all being. He is the absolute individual rather than the supreme universal. He is the One who said: "I Am That I Am" (Ex. 3:14 AV), meaning that he is the cause of his own existence. He is not an unmoved mover or World Soul that is incapable of fellowship, but rather as a triune being he has perfect fellowship within himself. Eckhart, Tillich, and many others who stand in the mystical tradition depict God as beyond existence, and yet Scripture tells us: "Whoever would draw near to God must believe that he exists and that he rewards those who seek him" (Heb. 11:6).

The *imago Dei* for the evangelical is not a divine spark within man, but rather a relationship between God and man perfectly exemplified in Jesus Christ. Man is related to God at the core of his being, and yet there is no part of man's being that is divine. As Kierkegaard stoutly affirms, biblical religion does not teach "the unity of the divine and the human" or "the identity of subject and

---

[21] Søren Kierkegaard, *The Sickness Unto Death* (trans. Walter Lowrie), (Princeton University Press, 1941), p. 207.

object."[22] In the mind of the Bible man is altogether a creature, and this means that he does not have a natural immortality, although Platonists often speak of the immortality of the soul. Whereas the mystics stress the continuity between God and man, the evangelicals speak of the discontinuity. Only God himself can bridge the infinite gulf which separates man from his Maker, and God has done this in the incarnation of Jesus Christ.

For evangelical theology Jesus is the Son of God incarnate in human flesh, not a deified or divine man. That he basically has his origin in God rather than in fallen humanity is attested by the Virgin Birth narratives. He is the Savior from sin rather than a world master or teacher. Through his death he satisfied the wrath of God and thereby paid the penalty for sin on behalf of the human race. The doctrine of the substitutionary atonement is one of the fundamentals of evangelical theology.

In evangelical piety faith signifies a divine-human encounter (Brunner). It is not being touched by mystery so much as being confronted by a living Savior. It is not naked assent, as John of the Cross sometimes envisages it, but rather a personal relationship between the trusting child and a loving Father. Faith moreover is not devoid of rational content, since God reveals himself to us by means of his Word. The evangelical experience or the experience of faith does not signify the complete transcendence of reason but rather the conversion and transformation of reason.

Revelation signifies not a moment of conscious insight but rather a divine incursion into human history. It is not "every new and original communication of the Universe to man" (Schleiermacher), but rather the incomparable, unrepeatable event of God becoming man in Jesus Christ. We find God not so much by looking into ourselves as by trusting in his revelation in Jesus Christ attested and mirrored in the Bible. The truth is not concealed in the natural self; rather it is revealed in the Word of God. As Brunner put it: "Faith . . . declares truth is in God's own Word alone; and what is in me is not truth."[23] Self-knowledge does not lead to God-knowledge, but rather God-knowledge makes self-knowledge possible.

---

[22] Søren Kierkegaard, *Concluding Unscientific Postscript* (trans. David F. Swenson), (Princeton University Press, 1944), p. 290.
[23] Emil Brunner, *The Word and the World* (London: SCM, 1931), pp. 76, 77.

Sin in evangelical piety does not signify negation or deprivation, a loss of something good *(deprivatio)*, but rather depravation, a wicked corruption *(depravatio)*. It is not an absence (Eckhart), nor a privation (Augustine), nor an estrangement from God (Dionysius), but rather a revolt of man against the will of God. Whereas the mystic views the antithesis as between spirit and nature, the evangelical sees it as between the holy God and man the sinner. For Luther sin consists not simply in concupiscence or lust but rather in a lust for power. The essence of sin lies in the spirit of man, not in his flesh, in hardness of heart, not in natural weakness. Tillich follows Plato in describing sin in terms of the transition from essence to existence, but sin is not a separate existence so much as distorted existence or enslaved existence.

Salvation in biblical prophetic religion consists essentially in forgiveness. It is not reunion with the ground of being but acceptance by a merciful Father. Salvation is also liberation — not from the moral body but rather from self-will and also the demonic powers of darkness. It is not equivalent to self-realization or enlightenment, as the mystics sometimes express it. On the contrary, it entails the crucifixion of the self, the death of the self. Mystics also use this terminology, but they frequently mean by it the death of the ego rather than of the sinful human will.

Grace in evangelical theology essentially means the favor of God, not a power infused into man by which he becomes divine. The believer is a repentant sinner, not a divinized being. Grace brings about man's conversion, not his deification. To be sure, grace has concrete effects in the life of man; he is empowered now to live a holy life. But as a sinner he remains always under grace, that is, under the mercy of God; he is not yet permeated by grace so that he has become like God.

The dominant emphasis in evangelical theology is not union with God but rather the new life in Christ. There is a strong ethical note in biblical religion which is noticeably lacking in all idealistic and mystical philosophy. It is obedience to the will of God rather than submersion into the being of God that is the paramount concern. In the words of Philip Spener: "The sum of Christianity is repentance, faith and new obedience. . . ."[24] Certainly this note can also be

24 Philip Spener, *Theologische Bedenken* (Halle: Waysen-Hauses, 1713), II, p. 685.

detected in many of the Christian mystics, and yet mysticism on the whole tends to subordinate ethical obedience to the pursuit of purely spiritual goals. Evelyn Underhill points to the other-worldly orientation of mysticism: "Its aims are wholly transcendental and spiritual. It is in no way concerned with adding to, exploring, rearranging, or improving anything in the visible universe."[25] The convergence of evangelicalism and mystical spirituality can be seen in the voluntaristic mysticism of Bernard of Clairvaux, Eckhart, and Teresa of Avila, in which man's will becomes a veritable instrument of the will of God. And yet even in these mystics the final goal is departure from this world and reunion with the Eternal.

Piety in evangelical theology is understood in terms of repentance and obedience under the cross. It consists not so much in a feeling of absolute dependence on God (Schleiermacher) or in contemplative adoration as in a lifelong struggle against sin and perseverance in conversion (Luther). It signifies not disengagement from the world but combat in the world and against the world. Partly because of this stress upon combat, the evangelical is prone to be more intolerant and exclusive than the mystic. The fact that evangelicals appeal to a particular and decisive revelation also accounts for their exclusiveness and their antipathy to eclecticism and syncretism.

The biblical and evangelical understanding of love is that of Agape rather than Eros. Agape signifies the love that does not seek its own, the sacrificial self-giving love of the cross. It is God's way to man, whereas Eros is man's way to God (Nygren). The significance of Agape love is nowhere better stated than in 1 John 4:10: "In this is love, not that we loved God but that he loved us and sent his Son to be the expiation for our sins." This conception of Agape was certainly foreign to Proclus and Dionysius, but it is not wholly absent from the mystical tradition.[26]

For the evangelical the stages on life's way consist of justification, sanctification, and glorification. The basis of our salvation lies in the justification of God, not in the seeking and striving of man. This is why evangelicals uphold so vigorously the doctrine of

[25] Evelyn Underhill, *Mysticism* (New York: E. P. Dutton, 1930), p. 81.
[26] Certainly Eros piety is transcended in these words of the *Theologia Germanica:* "We must not seek our own, neither in things spiritual nor in things natural." Ray Petry, ed., *Late Medieval Mysticism*, in *Library of Christian Classics* (London: SCM, 1957), XIII, p. 350.

justification by grace and contrast it with the works-righteousness that is rampant in much of popular mystical religion. Justification, of course, must be received by faith, and faith must bear fruit in works of love. But good works are the sign and confirmation of the justification that has already been procured for us by Christ.

Prayer in prophetic religion consists essentially in supplication. Adoration and thanksgiving are seen as elements of petitionary prayer (Karl Barth). Prayer is wrestling with God, not meditating upon God. It is an attempt to change God's will, not simply a passive resignation to God's will. It entails not the total renunciation of one's desires but the offering up of one's desires to God in the hope that they may be fulfilled in God's own way and time. It is the pouring out of the heart before God more than a lifting up of the mind to God. As Luther said: "To come to the Father" is not "to ascend as on wings to heaven, but with heartfelt confidence to commit oneself to Him as to a gracious Father."[27]

Christian mystics commonly point to Jesus himself as the example of one who practiced meditative and contemplative prayer. Yet a close examination of the prayer life of our Lord would seem to indicate that his prayers were definitely petitionary and intercessory in nature. He withdrew from human company not in order to extricate himself from the bonds of the flesh and become one with the Infinite but rather to bring his supplications before God and intercede for his fellowman in agony and sometimes in tears. Söderblom gives us this picture:

> So much we may know with absolute certainty from all the Gospel tells of Jesus, that his prayer never was merely a state of soul attained by some sure method, an *oratio mentalis*, a Prayer of Quiet, a meditation, but an intercourse and conversation with the heavenly Father, an outlet for anguish and uncertainty and for questions that needed answer; the bursting forth of a tone of jubilation, a trembling yet confident intimacy longing for undisturbed intercourse with the Father in Heaven, although the feeling of nearness and fellowship with him was wont never to cease during the duties and occupations of the day.[28]

---

27 Friedrich Heiler, *Prayer*, p. 156.
28 Nathan Söderblom, *The Living God* (Boston: Beacon, 1962), p. 59.

For the evangelical, proclamation is the primary means of grace. Christian obedience is also spoken of as a means by which the Spirit of God reaches us, but very little is said of meditation in this context. Evangelicals do not seek to give birth to God, as Eckhart describes it; rather their aim is to give testimony to God. Evangelism is the heartbeat of faith (Nels Ferré), and evangelism means the heralding of the good news of reconciliation and redemption. In Kierkegaard's view: "The communication of Christianity must ultimately end in 'bearing witness, . . .' For truth, from the Christian point of view, does not lie in the subject (as Socrates understood it) but in a revelation which must be proclaimed."[29]

Authentic mystics address their writings to a select company of adepts; mysticism is essentially esoteric. According to Heiler, "Mystics do not go into the streets to show the crowd their precious treasure which they have found after long seeking and struggling; they do not preach to the masses and they make no converts."[30] They seek companions in the quest for truth and sometimes even disciples, but they do not as a rule witness to an exclusive historical revelation. Several of the mystics, including Bernard of Clairvaux, Johann Tauler, and Meister Eckhart, were noted preachers, but for the most part they spoke to select audiences, cloistered monks and nuns. A few mystics whose devotional writings have had public appeal, such as Thomas à Kempis and William Law, intended their works only for individuals and small groups.

At the same time, we must not close our eyes to the great missionary movement within Catholicism associated with the names of such saints as Columba, Dominic, Raymond Lull, Francis Xavier, and Vincent Ferrer. It is a moot point to what extent the missionary preachers were inspired by an evangelical devotion grounded in Scripture or by the mystical spirituality of the medieval Catholic tradition. Heiler is indubitably right in affirming that the logic of mysticism tends against the heralding of an authoritative exclusive message, and yet this can be seen better in the monistic, pantheistic mysticism of the Orient than in Christian mysticism.

---

[29] Søren Kierkegaard, *The Journals of Søren Kierkegaard* (ed. and trans. Alexander Dru), (London: Oxford, 1951), p. 259.
[30] Heiler, *Prayer*, p. 161.

The orientation of evangelical piety is outward. We are called to fix our attention upon the God who stands over against us and who speaks to us through the events of sacred history and the pages of Scripture. It is not simply what the Spirit says to us within but what the Bible says that is regarded as supremely important. Luther expressed this very poignantly: "And this is the reason why our theology is certain: it snatches us away from ourselves and places us outside ourselves, so that we do not depend on our own strength, conscience, experience, person, or works but depend on that which is outside ourselves, that is, on the promise and truth of God, which cannot deceive."[31]

Evangelical theologians also speak of the inward testimony of the Spirit, and it would be misleading to suggest that their orientation is exclusively outward. Yet as John Bunyan, the Puritan spiritual writer, points out, the Christ within leads us to the Christ without:

> As for thy saying that salvation is Christ within, if thou mean in opposition to Christ without, instead of pleading for Christ thou wilt plead against him; for Christ, God-man, without on the cross, did bring in salvation for sinners; and the right believing of that justifies the soul. Therefore Christ within, or the Spirit of him who did give himself a ransom, doth not work out justification for the soul in the soul, but doth lead the soul out of itself and out of what can be done within itself, to look for salvation in that Man that is now absent from his saints on earth.[32]

The ideal in biblical prophetic religion is not simply withdrawal but withdrawal and return. Withdrawal from the world is encouraged for the purpose not of deepening spirituality but of equipping ourselves for service and mission in this world. In our prayers we do not become oblivious to the world, but rather we become ever more identified with the world in its agony and travail. Religious communities have a place in evangelical religion but only if grounded in the principle of greater availability for service to the unfortunate and needy in the world. Celibacy has been highly regarded by many of the saints in evangelical Christendom, but it is always seen as a

---

[31] Jaroslav Pelikan, ed. and trans., *Luther's Works* (St. Louis: Concordia, 1963), XXVI, p. 387.
[32] Thomas Kepler, ed., *The Spiritual Riches of John Bunyan* (Cleveland: World, 1952), p. 111.

practical means for service, not as inherently superior to marriage. The Herrnhut community, founded by Count Zinzendorf, illustrates the evangelical ideal in community life whereas the monastic kingdom of Mount Athos represents the ideal of mystical religion. Where the two types converge is in the sisters of mercy in Roman Catholicism and the deaconess orders in Protestantism.

THE MYSTICAL ELEMENT IN FAITH

One must not give the impression that biblical faith is devoid of a mystical element. Indeed, the opposite must be asserted, particularly over against the rationalistic orthodoxy that seeks to stifle all subjective feeling and enthusiasm. Faith consists not only in personal confidence in Christ but also in mystical participation in Christ. In John's Gospel we read that just as Christ is in the Father, so are we in him (Jn. 17). The illustration of the vine and the branches is given in order to point out the mystical, even ontological communion between Christ and his members (Jn. 15:1-6). Again in the Fourth Gospel Jesus tells us that we shall eat of his flesh and drink of his blood (6:52-58). In 2 Peter 1:4 it is affirmed that we can "become partakers of the divine nature." This is a text that is often appealed to by Eastern Orthodox mystics.

Paul often uses the metaphor "in Christ" to make clear the mystical dimension of authentic Christianity. He even contends that we are justified and sanctified "in Christ" (Gal. 2:17; 1 Cor. 1:2). He likens Holy Communion to a "participation" in the body and blood of Christ (1 Cor. 10:16). Yet Paul always seeks to relate the Christ in us *(Christus in nobis)* to the Christ for us *(Christus pro nobis)*. This can especially be seen in Galatians 2:20, which is often given as an example of "Christ-mysticism": "I have been crucified with Christ; it is no longer I who live, but Christ who lives *in* me; and the life I now live in the flesh I live by faith in the Son of God, who loved me and give himself *for* me" (italics added).

Karl Barth is very insistent that the subject-object relationship is maintained in the experience of faith. Radical mysticism seeks to dissolve this relationship. It is true that God's otherness must always be upheld even in the intimate union of faith; at the same time we must insist that the alienation, the radical apartness, the cleavage between God and man, is overcome in faith. God is no longer an object in faith, but a Subject, to be sure another Subject who enters into personal communion with the believer. We can say that the subject-object antithesis is surmounted in faith, but now there is a relationship between two subjects, God and man. There is no dissolution of personality, but rather losing oneself and finding oneself again in God. Dialectical theology often refers to the "I-Thou encounter," but biblical faith speaks also of the intimate communion, even union, between the I and the Thou. As one of the great hymns of Pietism expresses it:

> He is mine and I am His,
> Joined with Him in close communion;
> And His bitter passion is
> The foundation of this union.[33]

Bonhoeffer also discerned this mystical element in biblical faith: ". . . the Christian person achieves his true nature when God does not confront him as Thou, but 'enters into' him as I."[34]

Another truth in Christian mysticism is that revelation remains mysterious even to the believer. That we definitely encounter mystery in revelation is attested by Luther, who says, "The hardest of all things is faith in Christ, which is being rapt and translated from all things of sense, within and without, into those things beyond sense within and without, namely into the invisible, most high and incomprehensible God."[35] Karl Barth also points to the presence of mystery in Christian faith: "It is not God who stands before us if He does not stand before us in such a way that He is and remains a mystery to us. Mystery means that He is and remains the One whom we know only because He gives Himself to be known."[36] At the same time, it should be said that the revelation of God is not a pure mystery, as mystics generally would have us believe, but also a definite word concerning God's will and purpose for man. God's

---

[33] Christian Keymann, "Jesus Will I Never Leave," in *The Evangelical Hymnal* (St. Louis: Eden, 1922), p. 207.
[34] Dietrich Bonhoeffer, *Sanctorum Communio* (trans. R. Gregor Smith), (London: Collins, 1963), p. 37.
[35] *D. Martin Luther's Werke* (Weimar: Hermann Böhlaus Nachfolger, 1939), 57, 144, 10 (trans. Gordon Rupp).
[36] Karl Barth, *Church Dogmatics* (trans. T. H. L. Parker, *et al.*), (Edinburgh: T. & T. Clark, 1957), II, 1, p. 41.

Word is disclosed and veiled in the biblical testimony and the sacramental signs of the church. We never have divine content except in worldly form, and this means that it is always hidden but only partially so. Christian mystics are right in holding that the meaning of God's truth is veiled by mystery, but evangelicals rightly insist that this is a mystery illumined by meaning.

Neo-orthodox theology has deemphasized the role of religious experience in order to give more weight to the objectivity of God's saving action in history. And yet Christian mystics as well as many of the older evangelicals remind us that there is no salvation apart from the experience of faith. Luther affirms: "It is not enough that you say Luther, Peter, Paul have said so but you must experience Christ Himself in your own conscience and feel that it is unquestionably God's Word, though all the world opposes it."[37] Calvin maintains that it is not sufficient "to know Christ as crucified and raised up from the dead, unless you experience, also, the fruit of this. . . . Christ therefore is rightly known, when we feel how powerful his death and resurrection are, and how efficacious they are in us."[38] In evangelical biblical theology, religious experience is very necessary, but it must be said against mysticism in general that our faith is mediated through but not derived from experience. The source of our experience is the God who enters human experience from beyond, and this truth must never be obscured.

It is interesting to note that both mystics and evangelicals call us to walk by faith and not by sight. The Protestant Reformers were adamant that we place our trust not in our reason or senses but in God's promises declared in Scripture. Luther said that the main thing that distinguishes a Christian from a natural man is that the latter "sees, evaluates, and judges everything according to the old birth, according to what he sees or feels."[39] The Christian, on the other hand, "is not guided by what he sees or feels. . . . He remains with the testimony of Christ; he listens to Christ's words and follows Him into the darkness."[40] The Christian mystics also warn against a

---

[37] Quoted in Adolf Köberle, *The Quest for Holiness* (trans. John Mattes), (Minneapolis: Augsburg, 1938), p. 80.

[38] John Calvin, *Commentaries on the Epistles of Paul the Apostle to the Philippians, Colossians, and Thessalonians* (trans. John Pringle), (Edinburgh: Calvin Translation Society, 1851), p. 98.

[39] Jaroslav Pelikan, ed., *Luther's Works* (St. Louis: Concordia, 1957), XXII, p. 306.

[40] *Ibid.*

dependence upon reason and the senses. They are particularly distrustful of visions and extraordinary experiences. John of the Cross affirms: "Wherefore he that would . . . seek any vision or revelation, would not only be acting foolishly, but would be committing an offense against God, by not setting his eyes altogether upon Christ."[41] Eckhart contends that when Christians "increase in love, such experiences will come less facilely, and the love that is in them will be proved by the constancy of their fidelity to God, without such enticements."[42]

One major difference between mystics and biblical personalists is that the latter are unwilling to abandon all signs and confirmations of the truth of the gospel. Jesus said that no sign will be given, except one, namely, the sign of the resurrection (Mt. 12:39). The faith of the evangelical is grounded in the promises of Scripture and is not simply a leap in the dark. For the evangelical, faith is not without evidence; rather it provides its own evidence, namely, the assurance of forgiveness and the new life in the Spirit. The Christian is not like a blind man (cf. John of the Cross) but rather one who sees dimly, yet truly (1 Cor. 13:12). Moreover, he seeks to understand his faith and is not content with a feeling of beatitude or inner peace, with being "moved lovingly" by that which he does not know.[43]

Again it must be recognized that salvation consists in reunion with God as well as forgiveness. Justification is the foundation of our salvation, but certainly it is only the beginning of a process that must culminate in perfect sanctification and glorification. The early church fathers did not hesitate to speak of the "deification" of man; however, they did not have in mind the submersion of man in God but rather his transfiguration into the likeness of God. Reformation and neo-Reformation theologies are tempted to overplay the forensic aspect of justification, though this must always be taken seriously. Yet, as even Calvin affirmed, justification leads into and is

---

[41] In his *Ascent of Mount Carmel*, Bk. II, Ch. XXII, in *The Complete Works of Saint John of the Cross* (trans. and ed. E. Allison Peers), (4th ed., London: Burns, Oates & Washbourne, 1953), I, p. 163.

[42] Raymond Blakney, trans. and ed., *Meister Eckhart*, p. 14.

[43] The evangelical could not say as did one mystic: "Be willing to be blind, and give up all longing to know the why and how, for knowing will be more of a hindrance than a help. It is enough that you should feel moved lovingly by you know not what. . . ." *The Cloud of Unknowing*, p. 93.

fulfilled in sanctification, and the Christian mystics remind us of this truth.

The Reformers remained true to the Pauline emphasis by interpreting grace as the undeserved favor of God rather than a divine power or energy infused into man. At the same time, we must recognize that grace has concrete effects in our lives, and in this sense grace is also creative divine power within us. God not only declares us righteous, but he also makes us righteous by his Spirit. Evangelicals often speak of transforming grace, but do not we need to refer also to elevating grace (as do our Catholic brethren)? Man is not only restored to perfect manhood by God's grace but also elevated to God-man-hood. Is it not man's destiny to become a son of God (Mt. 5:45; Rom. 8:23)?

We also need to do justice to what many Christian mystics say about love. It is true that the biblical idea of love is that of God coming down to man in Jesus Christ. But is man's love totally denied? Is it not rather transformed and channeled in a new direction? Nygren, for example, finds himself unable to speak of man's love to God. He affirms only the love that is poured into us and which is then directed outward to our neighbor. But surely in the view of Jesus nothing is so important as loving God. What is evil is not Eros as such, but fallen Eros. Nygren holds that man can bring nothing to God except his sins, but cannot man bring love to God, cannot man give glory to God on the basis of the indwelling Spirit of God? Nygren regards with suspicion the idea of an ascent to God, but does not the Bible speak of both the eagle and the dove, the symbols for human ascent and divine descent? To be sure, we can ascend to the throne of grace only on the basis of grace, but many Christian mystics, and certainly church fathers such as Irenaeus, Athanasius, and Gregory of Nyssa, would also concur in this.

Whereas the goal of the Christian life is described by mystics as the beatific vision and perfect beatitude, in evangelical circles the emphasis is upon fellowship not only with God but with the whole company of the saints. The truth in Christian mysticism is that genuine fellowship has its basis in the union between the believer and his Lord and that the love of God takes priority over everything else. Yet it must also be insisted that love for God must overflow in love for one's neighbor. We are called not simply to personal sanctity but to social holiness (Wesley). Our goal is not only the vision of God but the holy city, the community of the blessed. It is this note that is often missing in the writings of the mystics.

Christian mystics are inclined to speak of Jesus more as the exemplar of piety than as the Savior from sin. Whenever the latter is lost sight of, we leave the Christian circle for an anthropocentric religion.[44] But it must be remembered that the mystical and moral influence theories of the atonement also have some truth and have many spokesmen in the catholic tradition of the church. Kierkegaard was right when he declared that Christ is both Savior and Example. To stress one to the detriment of the other propels us either in the direction of antinomianism or legalism. Contemporary Protestant theologians such as Regin Prenter, Anders Nygren, Karl Barth, and Emil Brunner look askance upon the *imitatio Christi*, but this is a doctrine that is solidly embedded in the New Testament (cf. Mt. 16:24; 1 Cor. 11:1; Eph. 5:1; 1 Pet. 2:21). The *imitatio Christi* does not mean that we should copy Christ in externals, but it does mean that we should be conformed to his image in the daily tasks of life. It is not a means of justification, but it is certainly a sign and confirmation of our justification. Moreover, it is the pathway of our sanctification and the road to glorification.

I have already discussed the two different approaches to prayer. With the Evangelical Reformers I hold that true prayer is essentially supplication and that adoration and thanksgiving spring out of as well as return to this. Yet is there not also a place for meditation and contemplation in Christian piety? The psalmist tells us that he meditates on the law of the Lord day and night (Ps. 1:2). Paul calls us to set our minds on things that are above (Col. 3:2) and to think about those things that are true and excellent and worthy of praise (Phil. 4:8). Such Protestant saints as Richard Baxter, Henry Scougal, and Jeremy Taylor, all of whom stand more or less in the Puritan tradition, had a high regard for meditation and encouraged its practice. Luther recommended heartfelt meditation upon the

---

[44] Fichte, whom Otto regards as a modern mystic, clearly moved outside the Christian circle when he wrote in criticism of the Reformation: "It was necessary not merely to change the external mediator between God and man but to require no external mediator at all, since the bond of unity with the divine is to be found within oneself." Johann G. Fichte, *Reden an die deutsche Nation*, in *Sämmtliche Werke*, Siebenter Band, Dritte Abteilung (Berlin: Verlag von Veit und Comp., 1846), p. 349.

passion of Jesus Christ. The danger appears when we come to regard meditation as a higher stage of prayer, whereas it is a spiritual discipline in its own right. It can strengthen prayer and prepare the way for authentic prayer. The convergence of the two types of spirituality in regard to prayer can be seen in Mother Basilea Schlink, the mother-superior of the Protestant Sisters of Mary. In her little book *The Weapon of Prayer* she says first of all that prayer is "to hold the Name of Jesus, the Name above every other name, continually and lovingly in our hearts." But then she goes on to affirm that prayer is "to plead before the Father the wounds of His only Son" and "to pour out our hearts to the Father with childlike trust in His love."[45] Basically her understanding of prayer is evangelical, but she has incorporated some mystical elements that are also present in the Bible.

I hold that the orientation of the biblical Christian will be both inward and outward. The Christian mystics place the accent upon the interior life whereas the Reformers and the neo-orthodox theologians of today seek to ground faith in the revelation in the Bible. It is interesting to note that the same apostle who proclaimed "God was in Christ reconciling the world to himself" (2 Cor. 5:19) also affirmed "Christ in you, the hope of glory" (Col. 1:27). The Christian faith holds to both the historical Christ and the indwelling Christ, the mystical Christ. At the same time, the mystical Christ directs us always to the biblical story of his sacrifice on the cross, but the Bible in turn points us again to the risen Christ who dwells within us by his Spirit. It must be said against many of the mystics that God is not to be identified with the depth of the soul but rather with the Spirit who is always apart from us even while he is within us. Tillich, despite his mystical bent, has rightly said: "If God speaks to us, this is not the 'inner word'; rather, it is the Spiritual Presence grasping us from 'outside.' But this 'outside' is above outside and inside; it transcends them."[46] Pascal also warned against a certain kind of introspection which often characterizes mysticism: "The Stoics say, 'Retire within yourselves; it is there you will find your rest.' And that is not true. . . . Happiness is

---

[45] See Mother Basilea Schlink, *The Weapon of Prayer* (Darmstadt-Eberstadt: Oekumenische Marienschwesternschaft, 1957).

[46] Paul Tillich, *Systematic Theology* (University of Chicago, 1963), III, p. 127.

neither without us nor within us. It is in God, both without us and within us."[47]

The mystics err when they locate authority in religious experience. And yet does not authority also have a mystical or perhaps we should say an experiential pole? The Reformers stressed the paradoxical unity of Word and Spirit, historical revelation and the inward experience of faith. I am not thinking here of the inner light understood as a divine immortal spark within man but rather of the transformed conscience, the inward illumination of the Holy Spirit. Certainly apart from this inner illumination faith would be a barren rationalism. Indeed is there not yet another pole of authority — the ecclesiastical or sacramental, the voice of the church? And within and beyond all of these relative authorities, which are mutually dependent, there is the transcendent Word of God, the living Christ, who alone is the absolute, unconditional authority.

The mysticism in the Bible might be called a "Savior mysticism," in that it signifies a communion with the living Christ rather than with the World Soul, the ground of being, or the undifferentiated Godhead. It might also be described as a "sacramental mysticism," for it is through the preaching of the Word conjoined with external signs — water, bread, and wine — that we are incorporated into and continue in the body of Christ. Such a mysticism is the complement rather than the antithesis to what we have called biblical personalism. Faith entails both encounter and communion, and the two are equally important.

Tillich has tried to do justice to the personalistic element in Christian mysticism in his distinction between a mysticism of love and a mysticism of dissolution. The first type, which is represented in the catholic tradition, seeks always to maintain individuality, since love heightens rather than destroys the personal. At the same time, Tillich has been unable to maintain this distinction in his own theology, for the logic of his position drives him beyond the personal. That a mysticism of love can lead to a mysticism of dissolution is illustrated also in Schleiermacher's theology; he too sought to maintain the personal element in faith, and yet he was not wholly successful. This can be seen in these words from his *Addresses:* "Would they but attempt to surrender their lives from

---

[47] Blaise Pascal, *Pensées and The Provincial Letters* (trans. W. F. Trotter and Thomas M'Crie), (New York: Random House, Modern Library, 1941), p. 154.

love to God! Would they but strive to annihilate their personality and to live in the One and in the All!"[48]

AREAS OF TENSION

Despite the presence of a mystical element in Christian faith, Christian mysticism as a movement and tradition has diverged from the biblical witness by making this element the criterion and ground of Christian thinking. Mystical experience has become the source and norm rather than the medium, fruit, and sign of Christian faith. Consequently there remain areas of tension between mystical theology and evangelical theology, and it is necessary to be cognizant of these particularly in view of the new ecumenical climate.

One doctrine that has been a barrier between biblical evangelicalism and Christian mysticism is the justification of the ungodly. For the mystics man is justified only insofar as he becomes righteous and holy. He is justified not on the basis of what he is declared to be in Christ but on what he might become through divine grace. This view is clearly expressed by the author of *The Cloud of Unknowing:* "For it is not what you are or have been that God looks at with his merciful eyes, but what you would be."[49] Even those mystics who adhere to a high doctrine of grace, such as Johann Tauler and the author of the *Theologia Germanica,* fail to grasp the forensic and paradoxical character of justification.[50] They see justification as being realized in the birth of God in the soul, not as an imputation of righteousness to those who are not deserving. But for Paul, and also for the Reformers, God justifies us while we are yet in our sins (Rom. 4:5; 5:6, 8). Luther spoke of our salvation being grounded in the *alien righteousness* of God, which signifies the merits of Jesus Christ and not our own worthiness. Mystics generally maintain that what is indispensable is personal holiness, our own righteousness. Thomas Merton comes close to the Reformation position when he

---

[48] Friedrich Schleiermacher, *On Religion* (trans. John Oman), (New York: Harper & Row, 1958), pp. 100, 101. For an unsympathetic evangelical critique of Schleiermacher's mysticism see Emil Brunner, *Die Mystik und das Wort,* 2nd aufl. (Tübingen: J. C. B. Mohr, 1928).
[49] *The Cloud of Unknowing,* p. 144.
[50] See Bengt Hägglund, "The Background of Luther's Doctrine of Justification in Late Medieval Theology," *Lutheran World,* VIII, no. 112 (June, 1961), pp. 24-46.

affirms: "If then we are to be holy, Christ must be holy in us. If we are to be 'saints,' he must be our sanctity."[51] Yet Merton is not speaking of forensic justification, the imputation of righteousness; moreover, he holds that the righteousness of Christ must be communicated to man before he is justified. The doctrine of the justification of the ungodly remains an area of tension between the two types of spirituality but perhaps not an insuperable barrier. Tillich diverges from the mystical tradition in his strong adherence to the Reformation doctrine of justification. For him this means that we are accepted despite the fact that we are unacceptable.

Another area of tension is the historical complexion of biblical, evangelical faith and the ahistorical orientation of mysticism. For mystics such as Eckhart the birth of the Son in the soul is more important than the historical incarnation of Jesus. Some of the Christian mystics have appealed to the historical only to illustrate some universal principle or idea. The crucifixion and the resurrection, for example, dramatize the death and rebirth of the soul. Those mystics who have sought to build upon the doctrine of the incarnation have been able to maintain the historical character of the faith in conjunction with its essentially nontemporal quality.

Perhaps the prime difference between the two kinds of spirituality is that mysticism seeks a God beyond and outside of the personal. Tillich speaks of the God who transcends the divine-human encounter. Eckhart refers to God as the Not-being who is the ground and source of all being. According to Bonaventura, "His center is everywhere, and His circumference nowhere." God, of course, is not a being besides others but the uncreated being who infinitely transcends all created being. But this must mean that God is wholly personal and not less than personal nor above the personal. Mysticism places the accent upon the immanence of God whereas deism upholds the radical transcendence of God. But the God of the Christian faith is both transcendent and immanent. He is the God whom the highest heaven cannot contain (1 Kings 8:27) and yet also the One who is in and through all things (Eph. 4:6). Many of the Christian mystics speak of identification rather than of identity with God and come to a position that might be better termed "panentheism" than "pantheism." In the former, the world is in God and God is in the world, but God is not the world nor the self.

---

[51] Thomas Merton, *Life and Holiness* (New York: Herder & Herder, 1963), p. 72.

Yet is not the Christian position a "supernatural creationism" whereby God brings the world (and the soul) into being out of nothing and enters into the world only because of love, not out of metaphysical necessity? Panentheism tends to make God and the world mutually dependent, whereas the God of the Bible can very well exist apart from the world and the self.

Evangelicalism is oriented about Holy Scripture; Christian mysticism emphasizes the inward testimony and light of the Holy Spirit. But are not both emphases needed for the full biblical and catholic faith? If we have the Spirit without the letter we end in spiritualism or philosophical mysticism *(Mysticismus)*.[52] If we have the letter apart from the Spirit we end in a rationalistic biblicism or confessionalism.

Similarly do not we need both Martha and Mary as types of the life of service and the religious life (cf. Lk. 10:38-42)? It is interesting to observe that Eckhart places Martha above Mary, since in his view the former represents the culmination of contemplation, which is loving service. Although holding to the ideal of contemplative adoration, Teresa of Avila maintains that Marthas are also necessary and that it is possible to be holy without being contemplative. Thomas Aquinas regards contemplation as higher than action, but he avers that here on earth the combination of the two types is preferable to the purely contemplative life. Is there not a place for brothers and sisters in community who intercede for the world in prayer as well as prophets, teachers, and evangelists?

If we are true to Scripture we must recognize that Jesus gives preference to Mary rather than to Martha. It was Mary who did the one thing needful, namely, to sit at the feet of the Master and hear the Word of God. Yet against the general tradition of mysticism I hold that Mary was not in contemplation as such; rather she was listening to the teaching of Christ. Is not this what is most important — the hearing and reading of the Word of God, and does not this take precedence over both contemplation and action? Faith comes by hearing (Rom. 10:17), and works of love as well as prayer are the fruits and consequences of living faith.

---

[52] Rudolf Otto and others have drawn the distinction between *Mystik*, meaning mysticism as a spiritual experience, and *Mysticismus*, which refers to mysticism as a philosophy of life. The Christian faith is irrevocably opposed to the latter but not necessarily to the former.

What is needed is a rediscovery of the mystical elements already in the Bible rather than a synthesis of biblical faith with Neo-Platonic idealism (as in medieval mysticism) or Spinozistic pantheism (as in the early Schleiermacher) or Oriental mysticism (as in Gerald Heard). We need to recover the doctrine of the mystical union between the believer and his Lord which was already very much present in Calvin and in the older Reformed tradition. Indeed, how can we understand or proclaim the gospel apart from spiritual communion with the crucified and risen Savior? How can we bring the Word to an unbelieving world unless we are indwelt by the Word through his Spirit? Yet we must take care to distinguish this mystical union (*unio mystica*), which lies at the heart of the Christian faith, from the experience of the undifferentiated unity of all things that characterizes the perennial philosophy of monistic mysticism. For the Christian encounters not the "mystical void" or the "wayless abyss" or the "nothingness" of existentialism but rather the living Savior, Jesus Christ.

Eight

A THEOLOGY OF
CHRISTIAN COMMITMENT

T HEOLOGIES TODAY SEEM to be taking shape on the basis of their
  approach to the relation of the sacred and the secular, the holy
and the profane. One aspect of this problem is how theology is to be
distinguished from secular philosophy. The crucial issue in this
whole discussion is the precise relationship between the church and
the world, the city of God and the city of man.

CHRIST AND CULTURE

Roman Catholic theologians have tried to relate the sacred and the
secular through a synthesis in which the secular finds its fulfillment
in the sacred. This approach was enunciated by Thomas Aquinas,
who interpreted reality in terms of a hierarchy of levels — nature,
grace, and glory. Just as grace builds upon and perfects nature, so
glory signifies the culmination of grace. Just as reason is completed
by revelation, so philosophy is completed by theology. This type of
theology fails to give serious enough attention to the brokenness and
sinfulness of human reason and culture. In the mind of the Bible
revelation signifies the overthrow and conversion of reason rather
than its fulfillment.

   In the circles of Reformation orthodoxy, paticularly Lutheranism, we find the theory of the two kingdoms, the kingdom of Christ

and the kingdom of the world, which remain at enmity until the end of time. The Christian is a member of both kingdoms and must seek to live out his calling in the world while at the same time giving absolute homage to Jesus Christ who stands over against the world. H. Richard Niebuhr has termed this position "Christ-and-culture-in-paradox."[1] Bultmann's existentialist theology also mirrors this general approach. The chief criticism of this view is that it tends to reinforce the cultural status quo. By dividing Christ and culture, the way is opened for interiorized religion.

Many theologians are presently tempted to identify the sacred and the secular. The new secular theology as represented by such men as J. A. T. Robinson, William Hamilton, and Harvey Cox would place the accent upon the identification and solidarity of the Christian with the world. All lines between the holy and the profane are erased, since the whole world is claimed as the domain of God. The coming kingdom of God is equated with the new metropolis or the secular city. The natural theology of men like Cobb and Ogden would also tend to blur the distinctions between Christ and culture, church and world. In their thinking God becomes a creative reconciling process within nature and society. The deficiency in the foregoing theologies is that they lose sight of the transcendent holy God of the Bible who stands over against the world of his creatures and brings their fallacious and idolatrous dreams and plans to naught. These theologies also fail to do justice to the presence of the demonic in modern technological mass culture.

Paul Tillich speaks in terms of a sacred-secular correlation. In his view the Christian faith answers the creative questions of the secular culture. The "Spiritual Community" includes both the church and the world. The world is the Spiritual Community in its latency. The world seeks for and moves toward that which is manifest in the fellowship of faith. In his theology the distinction between faith and unbelief is only relative. The power of the new aeon or the New Being, according to Tillich, is manifest in Jesus Christ to a superlative degree, but any person or even any thing can become a symbol of this reality. Therefore the whole world can be regarded as sacramental, that is, capable of revealing and bearing the New Being.

---

[1] See H. Richard Niebuhr, *Christ and Culture* (New York: Harper, 1951).

The strategy of withdrawal and separation is present in the circles of an ultraconservative evangelicalism as well as in such neo-Anabaptist groups as the Society of Brothers. These people retreat to an entrenched and outdated position that is accepted uncritically and sometimes even fanatically. The restorationist or traditionalist movement within Roman Catholicism also reflects this line of thinking. Separatist Christians succeed in drawing hard and fast lines between the church and world, but in the process they lose sight of the sinfulness within the church and also the working of the Holy Spirit in the world.

Finally we have today the rise of a new Social Gospel which typifies what H. Richard Niebuhr calls "Christ-transforming-culture." The theologians associated with *Renewal* magazine can certainly be placed in this category. This includes Harvey Cox, although he stands partly in the camp of culture Christianity.[2] Cox speaks of waging warfare against the remnant of evil which still exists in the world even after the victory of Christ. The locus of revelation in his theology is secular events of social change; the arena of salvation is the present struggle for social and racial equality. This approach more than the others can be commended for taking seriously the conflict and tension between the claims of the Christian faith and the values of a secular culture. On the other hand the danger in this movement is that it undercuts the radical uniqueness of the revelation in the Bible and the once-for-all character of the saving work of God in Jesus Christ. Too many preachers in this camp end in preaching the ideology of democracy or the Great Society rather than the gospel of the cross.

NEED AGAIN FOR DIASTASIS

The foregoing approaches all prove to be lacking in some significant area, even though each has much to commend it. They tend to result either in capitulation to the culture or in compromise beyond the point of no return. Even in reactionary and separatist theologies we find compromise through isolation from the disciplines of culture.

---

[2] James Gustafson has made this astute comment on Harvey Cox's theology: "What is, I believe, intended to be an ethic of 'Christ transforming culture' slips easily into an ethic of 'Christ of Culture'." Daniel Callahan, ed., *The Secular City Debate* (New York: Macmillan, 1966), p. 15.

Though these theologians often utilize disciplines such as the natural sciences for apologetic purposes, there is in reality no genuine openness to findings that call into question certain tenets of Christian piety: for example, the historicity of the Adamic fall. We find modern theology tending either toward syncretism (as in the case of Tillich and Robinson) or toward ghettoism (as in the case of Van Til or the Roman Catholic C. H. Duggan).

There is a need today to sharpen the lines between the church and the world. The reason is that the church is steadily becoming more acclimated to the culture, and it must seek to redefine its true nature if it is to resist total secularization. The answer to the problem of secularism, however, lies not in withdrawal but in attack. The point of contact with the world must be viewed as a point of conflict. The demonic and pulverizing forces within society must be challenged and defeated before they imperil the freedom of the Word of God in the pulpit. Karl Barth held that there was a need for *diastasis* or separation in the conflict between the Confessing Church and the National Socialists. The German Christians were the syncretists or culture-Christians of that period. Modern culture is no longer menaced by Nazism and fascism, but new secular salvations have arisen that are claiming the loyalties of men and women.[3] Among these are the new nationalism, dialectical materialism (which is by no means in a state of demise as some cultural analysts contend), secular humanism, one manifestation of which is the ideology of democracy, and the new hedonism, which represents a repristination of the ancient gods of fertility and sex.[4] Although we are supposedly living in a post-religious era, we are today witnessing the recrudescence of ever more virulent forms of idolatry and fanaticism. Against these political and secular religions the church must pronounce an unequivocal No.

It is to be acknowledged that the present mood of Western culture is relativistic and even nihilistic. The dominant philosophies including analytic philosophy, existentialism, and psychoanalysis all reflect the enervating spirit of relativism. Emil Brunner was right

---

[3] See Ernest B. Koenker, *Secular Salvations* (Philadelphia: Fortress, 1965).

[4] It is interesting to note that both Wm. Hamilton and Altizer view sex as the new domain of the sacred. See William Hamilton, "The Death of God," in *Playboy* (August, 1966), pp. 138, 139; Thomas Altizer and Wm. Hamilton, *Radical Theology and the Death of God* (Indianapolis: Bobbs-Merrill, 1966), pp. 178-180.

when he described the religious situation of Western man as being a
"metaphysical vacuum." But it is precisely this kind of climate that
breeds new and more monstrous idols such as the titanic gods of
nation, race, and hero. Modern culture has been depicted as the
society of the mass man, the other-directed man, the man who
receives his cues, his ideals, and his values from the mass culture.
Such a man is indeed an easy prey to totalitarianism of every kind.

In the secular, nihilistic age in which we live there is a peculiar
need for a Christian style of life, a life arrayed against the values and
goals of the culture. But such a life must be lived not apart from but
in the culture as a sign and witness of the coming kingdom of God.
The church should once again sound the call to sainthood. But what
is needed are not "secular saints" as William Hamilton avers, but
rather men and women who have drawn close to the mystical
wellsprings of the faith in prayer and devotion. The modern age
calls for "images of perfection" (Tillich) that radiate the light and
glory of the eternal God-Man, Jesus Christ. In this relativistic
period there is a need for a theology that is fully anchored in the
Word of God, which stands in judgment upon every philosophy and
ideology, including the American Way of Life. Yet a theology of the
Word must be supplemented by a theology of commitment or
devotion if what God has done in the past is to be made effectual in
the present.

BEYOND NEO-ORTHODOXY

The neo-orthodox theology associated with Karl Barth, Reinhold
Niebuhr, and Emil Brunner can be appreciated for its recovery of
the uniqueness of Jesus Christ and the authority of the biblical
revelation. The lines between the holy God and the secular culture
were drawn quite sharply in the original theology of crisis, although
Barth later placed the accent on the identification of God with
humanity. Barth's view that all people are in Christ whether they
realize it or not tends to mitigate the differences between the church
and the world. He maintains that all people are in the kingdom by
virtue of the triumph of Jesus Christ, although he will not say that
all people are in the covenant community. Yet in his theology the
lines between faith and unfaith, church and world, are considerably
blurred. This is not to deny Barth's very real concern for the life of

discipleship and his insistence that such a life should entail both service in and conflict with the world. Reinhold Niebuhr speaks of a hidden Christ who is present wherever men and women commit themselves to social righteousness. His distinction between the children of light and the children of darkness is made not on the basis of whether people have faith but on whether they have social concern. His view that the righteous are still sinners and that sinners are partly righteous contains much truth; yet the way it is stated serves to call into question the radical character of the new birth and the Christian life.

Another deficiency among neo-orthodox theologians is that they generally fail to maintain the inseparable connection between the saving work of God in Jesus Christ and a life of repentance and faith. For the most part they follow the dominant view of the Protestant Reformation, which regarded the Christian life as an effect or fruit of salvation rather than its precondition. Karl Barth goes still further in contending that our salvation has already been accomplished in the life and death of Jesus Christ and that faith is simply an acknowledgment of this fact. In the secular age in which we live it is well for us to reaffirm the Scriptural truth that the Christian life is more than a sign or fruit of salvation; it is a vital element in our salvation, although not its basis or source. It is the battlefield on which our salvation is fought for and recovered. We must hold that those who refuse to enter upon the life of costly discipleship are imperiling their salvation.

THE NEED FOR CHRISTIAN LIFE

Against that kind of Reformed theology that speaks only of extrinsic justification, I maintain that salvation is realized in both the work of God and the decision of man. Its locus is both the cross of Christ and the Christian life. Indeed, salvation cannot be said to have occurred apart from the obedience of faith. My viewpoint approaches that of modern secular theology which places the accent upon the decision and commitment of the believer. But whereas secular theologians speak of the arena of salvation as the present struggle for social justice, I envisage it as the daily crisis of repentance and faith, one that is grounded in and indeed rises out of the crisis of the death and resurrection of Jesus Christ. In my view, the conversion of the individual is prerequisite for the reformation of society. But this conversion refers not simply to a first decision for Christ but rather to the lifelong struggle to remain true to the faith into which we were baptized. Nor do I view conversion as adequate in itself. It must give rise to and be supplemented by social action if Christians are to remain true to their vocation.

In contradistinction to the new secular theology I hold that Christian life is not to be separated from Christian faith. The life of the Christian will be a life characterized not only by self-giving service but also by prayer and devotion. It will be a life grounded in and sustained by daily repentance before the cross of Jesus Christ. There cannot be such a thing as "religionless Christianity" if this means a Christianity without piety and inwardness. Still less can there be a "godless Christianity" which views Jesus only as the exemplary man rather than God incarnate.

In a theology of Christian commitment revelation consists in the conjunction of the outward hearing of the Scriptural word and the inward movement of the Spirit, awakening people to the truth of what is revealed. The message of revelation is none other than the gospel of free grace procured for us by the sacrificial life and death of Jesus Christ. This is to say a theology of Christian life or commitment will also be an evangelical theology. But it will be not a narrow conservative evangelicalism but rather a catholic evangelicalism — one that seeks to relate the gift of free salvation to the works and means of grace. I hold that our conversion must be rooted in Holy Baptism, and it must be nurtured by Holy Communion.

In contrast to the mainstream of current Protestant thought I maintain that the Christian life must be viewed as being integrally related to salvation. Salvation is here understood not as humanization and rehabilitation, as sociologists understand these terms, but rather as justification and sanctification. Yet against Rome I hold that the Christian life does not earn or merit salvation; rather it is a means of appropriating the salvation procured by Jesus Christ once for all times.

GODLINESS IN THE WORLD

This approach has a certain affinity with Reformed and Lutheran Pietism in its early stages. It also reflects the social-oriented evangelicalism of such pioneering spirits of the last century as the Blumhardts, Christian Spittler, and Wilhelm Loehe. My position diverges from radical pietism or spiritualism in that I seek to ground personal piety in the Word of God as proclaimed in the church and to relate it always to life in the world. It can be seen that I favor a piety that is *world-concerned* as well as *God-centered*. This kind of piety is neither divorced from life in the world nor completely immersed in the world. It makes a place for individual salvation and social holiness and seeks to relate both to the service of the glory of God.

My view approaches that of John Calvin, who was profoundly concerned with personal salvation and yet at the same time envisaged a holy community. For Calvin the claims of Christ are present in the public as well as in the private sphere of life. In his mind Christian piety is oriented not simply about the state of one's soul but rather about the glory of God and the advancement of his kingdom. And yet he rightly insisted that God is never more glorified than when we work out our salvation with fear and trembling. A theology of the glory of God will consequently also be a theology of Christian commitment and devotion.

The mission of the church is to serve the glory of God through the exaltation of Jesus Christ before the world. Christ calls his church to service and warfare in the secular world, but the roots and goals of the church are in the sacred: that is, in the realm of the spirit. Moreover, the church is to serve not the world as such but rather God in the world. I advocate not "worldly holiness" (J. A. T. Robinson) but rather a godliness that is lived out in the world. It is the service of Jesus Christ and not simply the service of mankind that should occupy our attention. As P. T. Forsyth so cogently expresses it: "The largest and deepest reference of the Gospel, is not to the world or its social problems, but to Eternity and its social obligations."[5] But these social obligations are precisely ministry in the world. The love of Jesus Christ certainly entails love for our neighbor. Worship that is done in spirit and in truth will invariably drive us to the service of our fellowman. But the primary motivation in our service is to glorify God out of gratefulness for what he has done for us in Jesus Christ.

---

[5] P. T. Forsyth, *The Church and the Sacraments*, 2nd ed. (London: Independent Press, 1947), p. 24.

Unlike the new secular theology I do not uphold the new morality, which makes love the only criterion for action. Rather, I favor evangelical obedience, which seeks always to relate love to the revealed law of Holy Scripture. At the same time, I do not wish to be associated with the legalistic morality that has been the hallmark of a latter-day puritanical Protestantism. The law is not a means to salvation, nor is it an inflexible standard. It must be interpreted in the light of the love of Jesus Christ, but it must never be lightly set aside in the name of this love. It is not an absolute criterion but a sure and dependable guide to conduct. I believe in relating the principles of the law and gospel to the existential situation in which people find themselves. But this cannot be considered "situation ethics" in the full sense of this term, in that I do not abandon principles but utilize them in the service of the glory of God and our fellow humanity. Instead of situation ethics I uphold an ethics of the law and gospel in which love is seen as fulfilling and not overthrowing the moral law of God. The proper focus is given in 1 John: "For this is the love of God, that we keep his commandments" (5:3; cf. Jn. 14:15; 1 Cor. 7:19; 1 Jn. 2:5; 2 Jn. 6). The goal of an evangelical ethics is morality, not simply maturity.

THE COMING KINGDOM

In the area of eschatology I hold that the object of man's hope is not the new metropolis nor the Great Society, but the holy community. This holy community can be approximated in this world, but it will not be established in its perfection until the end of world history. The kingdom of God has already been inaugurated, but it will not be perfected within the confines of history, since our world is marked for eventual destruction. In my view, although Christ has overthrown the demonic powers, they still rule in the world, and this world, that is, the old aeon, will finally pass away. This world will always be a battleground between the kingdom of God and the kingdom of darkness. The church will always be a colony of heaven in a hostile world. God's kingdom is to be associated with a new heaven and a new earth. Moreover, it will be manifested in God's time and in his own way. We can set up signs of this coming kingdom, but we cannot prepare the way for its coming. We cannot build the eternal kingdom, but we can pray and hope for its realization. We can herald its coming by working now for social righteousness, and yet all orders and communities in this world will have to perish when God creates his world anew (Bonhoeffer).

Since the kingdom of God ultimately lies beyond history, the Christian life is one of pilgrimage. We can anticipate and approximate the goal of perfect love, but we can never finally arrive in this life. Ours is a theology of wayfarers *(theologia viatorum)*. We must always be seeking to make our holiness perfect, and yet we can never extricate ourselves from the ambiguities and contradictions of human life while still in the flesh.

WORD AND LIFE

I seek to hold together two different approaches to culture: the separatist and the conversionist. Christians are to be inwardly separated from the evil of the world, and yet they should work for the conversion of broken people and the reform of perverse social structures in the world. I advocate not physical or monastic withdrawal as a general strategy but rather an interior life of devotion — what Bonhoeffer called an arcane or hidden discipline. Our prayer life must give rise to active involvement in the concerns of the world. This involvement should be expressed in social action as well as in charity to our neighbor. It should also take the form of proclamation. We are to be not only servants but also heralds of the message of salvation. Just as the basis of the Christian life is the hearing of the gospel, so one of its primary fruits should be the preaching of the gospel.

In a theology that is oriented about the biblical call to discipleship, word and life must both be viewed as indispensable. Indeed the post-modern secular man should be confronted not only by the proclamation of the Christian message but also by the demonstration of a Christian life. I hold with the Heidelberg Catechism that a "godly walk" can also be a potent means of grace (Question 86). Yet in contradistinction to the secular or radical theologians I must insist that a Christian style of life cannot take the place of evangelical, kerygmatic preaching. We must finally recognize that no life, not even that of the greatest saint, can bring people the assurance of forgiveness that is so desperately needed. The one thing needful is to wait upon and hear the Word of God, the message of salvation through the shedding of the blood of Jesus Christ. But our hearing must bear fruit in a life lived under the cross of Christ; otherwise our faith will wither away and die. The life of faith and love proceeds from the Word of God, and yet this Word will be withheld from us unless we continue in faith.

As the church faces the final decades of the twentieth century, it needs again to sound the call to total commitment to the living Savior, Jesus Christ. And such a commitment entails conflict with the pagan gods and ideologies of modern secular culture. The temptation today is to seek a rapprochement with the spirit of the age. But this is an attempt to gain relevance at the expense of theological integrity. Forsyth has rightly declared that "Christianity can endure, not by surrendering itself to the modern mind and modern culture, but rather by a break with it: the condition of a long future both for culture and the soul is the Christianity which antagonizes culture without denying its place."[6] By consecrating ourselves to the Lord and Judge of secular culture, we help to preserve its relative autonomy. By denying the arrogant presumption of the secular spirit, we point the children of this age to the One who alone can free us from the tyranny of false absolutes.

[6] P. T. Forsyth, *Positive Preaching and the Modern Mind*, 4th ed. (London: Independent Press, 1953), p. 89.

Nine

THE PILGRIMAGE OF FAITH

THE THEME THAT constantly reappears in evangelical spirituality is that the Christian life is one of pilgrimage. This note can also be discerned in Catholic and Eastern Orthodox piety, but perhaps it is more pronounced among evangelicals because of their view that there is a basic discontinuity between God and man and between the kingdom of God and the institutional church. For the evangelical the Christian life is a life of faith, and this means that salvation is not primarily a possession but a hope. And yet salvation is not exclusively hope or expectation; it is also a present experience, even though this experience is only an anticipation or foreshadowing of the glory that is to come.

In this chapter I shall seek to relate the evangelical understanding of faith to the ever recurring quest for signs and evidences of the reality of God and the supernatural. In my view the evangelical conception of faith is authentically catholic, since it is imbedded in the tradition of the universal church. Moreover, the category of "evangelical" includes many of those in the Roman Catholic communion who uphold the doctrine of salvation by the free grace of God and the necessity to live and walk by faith alone.

Two Types of Theology

In the history of theology two general theological types can be detected, although it is a separate question whether they are mutually exclusive. On the one hand, there is the theology of the cross *(theologia crucis)*, which depicts this life as a pilgrimage through a vale of tears. The sole guidepost is the gospel itself, which can be discerned only by faith. On the other hand, there is the theology of glory *(theologia gloriae)*, which holds that eternal life begins in the present and that Christians are already in heavenly places. According to this mentality, it is possible to experience now the bliss and rapture of the kingdom. Whereas the first type of theology speaks of the infinite distance between God and man, the second is oriented around the divine transformation of man. In the theology of the cross grace is a power *over* or *toward* man; in the theology of glory grace is a power *in* man. The theology of the cross places the accent on pilgrimage and the righteousness of faith. The theology of glory is inclined to stress the spiritual gifts and entire sanctification. The theology of the cross in its most consistent formulation is a theology of the Word of God, whereas the theology of glory is very probably more a theology of religious experience. Both types of theology might very well develop into finalized systems, but the theology of the cross because of its emphasis on the brokenness and helplessness of man is more likely to be a theology of the pilgrim and the sinner *(theologia viatoris et peccatoris)*. This note can be clearly perceived in Reformed piety, but it is also present in Catholic mystical thought; it is particularly evident today in such ecumenical Roman Catholic theologians as Karl Rahner and Hans Küng.[1]

It is, of course, wrong to separate these two types of theology, for the church must hold to both the cross and the resurrection, to futuristic as well as to realized eschatology. Moreover, faith itself is an experience as well as trust. Faith *(pistis)* has not only rational and volitional dimensions but also a mystical dimension. Faith is something other than a bare intellectual assent or a leap in the dark. Faith is basically an experience of the forgiveness and transforming power of Christ, although this experience must be carried forward

---

[1] The term theology of pilgrims *(theologia viatorum)* is much more Protestant than Catholic, but in traditional Catholic thought the distinction is often made between a theology on the way *(theologia in via)* and a theology in the homeland *(theologia in patria)*, and the latter is said to be possible only in the state of glory

and fulfilled in trust and obedience. Tillich's definition of faith as an ecstatic state of being grasped by the Spiritual Presence of God can be accepted as referring to one pole or aspect of faith.[2]

At the same time faith is not sight, and this is where some of those who adhere only to a theology of glory are likely to go astray. Faith is rooted in experience, to be sure; however, this is not sense experience, but a mystical experience that transcends the senses and even reason itself. It is an experience that cannot be prepared for or engendered by any effort or determination on our side. Faith and the capacity to receive faith are gifts of God. A theology based upon faith alone and not on sight or natural reason will consequently be a theology of revelation *(theologia revelata)*, not a natural theology. But the revelation that is the ground of faith is not a private revelation but the revelation of Jesus Christ in the history attested to in Holy Scripture. The experience of faith is integrally related to and mediated through the biblical witness concerning the historic Jesus and his work of redemption. Faith ought therefore to be regarded as a union of spiritual immediacy and historical mediacy (Emil Brunner).

It must be recognized that the ultimate source of faith is the Word of God, not the experience. Faith might be likened to drinking water from a well. We do not have the water until we receive it with our lips from a cup or glass, but the source of the water is the well, which can be said to correspond to the Word. Faith as a living or concrete reality begins in experience, but the truth-content of faith is grounded in the eternal Word of God, although this truth is mediated by experience. P. T. Forsyth has put it this way:

> The experimental religion of true faith is not based on experience, but on revelation and faith. It is *realized* by experience, it proceeds in experience; but it does not proceed *from* experience. Experience is its organ, but not its measure, not its principle. What we experience we possess, but faith is our relation not to what we possess, but to what possesses us. Our faith is not in our experience, but in our Saviour.[3]

---

[2] Paul Tillich, *Systematic Theology* (University of Chicago, 1963), III, p. 130ff. It is to be noted that Tillich understands ecstasy as self-transcending as opposed to emotionally intoxicating or exciting. The use of "ecstatic" and "ecstasy" in this chapter includes both connotations.

[3] P. T. Forsyth, *Christian Perfection*, in his *God the Holy Father* (London: Independent Press, 1957), p. 108.

The truth in the *theologia gloriae* is that in faith we really experience the presence of Christ; indeed, we become united with this presence. But the authentic insight in the *theologia crucis* is that what is experienced is not Christ in the fullness of his glory but Christ concealed in the creatureliness of the inner self and in the worldliness of the sacramental signs and witnesses of his redemption. Faith is therefore an indirect rather than a direct knowledge of God. It is a "knowing" in the midst of "unknowing." Faith signifies an encounter with mystery, but it is a mystery illuminated by the uncreated light of Christ.

The *theologia crucis* reminds us also that the truth of faith exceeds the limitations of our reason and can be grasped only in the form of paradox and mystery. But the *theologia gloriae* calls to our attention the fact that revelatory knowledge, despite its transcendence of human reasoning, does not contradict the essential structure of reason. The truth of faith, although not a datum of general experience or an axiom of reason, is nevertheless not arational or irrational. On the contrary, it is rational in the truest sense. Karl Barth has declared: "Christian faith is the illumination of the reason in which men become free to live in the truth of Jesus Christ and thereby to become sure also of the meaning of their own existence and of the ground and goal of all that happens."[4] The truth of faith signifies a structure of meaning that is capable of penetrating and re-orienting human thinking, although it can never be assimilated by the processes of thought. This truth, if it is to become a meaningful reality in our lives, must be received by a converted heart and mind, and it must be explicated by a reborn reason. To walk by faith alone means to walk in the light of the Eternal Logos, the reason and wisdom of God. To live on the basis of faith alone means to live on the basis of a reason that has been liberated from its bondage to self-will and is now being restored to its pristine unity with the Word.

---

[4] Karl Barth, *Dogmatics in Outline* (trans. G. T. Thomson), (New York: Philosophical Library, n.d.), p. 22. Barth goes on to affirm: "Christian faith is not irrational, not anti-rational, not supra-rational, but rational in the proper sense" (p. 23). My objection to Barth's position is that he emphasizes the Word to the detriment of mystery, although he acknowledges that the rational does not exhaust the reality of faith.

Although only the eyes of faith can perceive the truth of faith, it does not follow that the presence and work of God in nature and culture remain totally invisible. Once the reason of man is transformed and illuminated by the grace of God, reason—that is, faithful reason—can perceive the signs and evidences of the working of God in nature and even secular history. God is at work everywhere purifying and renewing his creation, but this work can be discerned only by those who have eyes to see and ears to hear. This is to say that the signs and wonders and mighty works of God can be perceived only by the person of faith. Faith is characterized by certainty but not clarity. Faithful reason is still not reason totally restored. We can know, but only brokenly and anticipatorily. The person of faith will humbly recognize that the synoptic or absolute perspective belongs to God alone.

The tension between a theology of the cross and a theology of glory can especially be seen in Paul's theology. Paul affirms the Christian life as both a struggle of faith and a new creation of God. But in his mind these are not diametrically opposed; they are complementary. Regeneration does not mean glorification, but the beginning of a process of conversion that will forever remain incomplete in this life. Now we have the first fruits of the Spirit, that is, the assurance and hope of salvation, but salvation in its fullness is still to be attained. Even the converted man is separated from God by his mortal frame and sinful will. He can trust and obey through the power of the indwelling Spirit, but he cannot yet see. This insight is cogently expressed by Paul: "So we are always of good courage; we know that while we are at home in the body we are away from the Lord, for we walk by faith, not by sight" (2 Cor. 5:6, 7). It is Paul's view that, despite the fact that there might be little evidence for the presence of God, we can know by faith that God is certainly with us. The Christian must remember that while he is in the earthly body, he is separated from God. Because of man's creatureliness and also his sinfulness, he cannot perceive the glory and majesty of God. Therefore the Christian must be content to walk by faith and not by the light of his own reason. And what is faith? It is, in the words of an apostle who stands in the Pauline tradition, "the assurance of things hoped for, the conviction of things not seen" (Heb. 11:1). It is knowledge of Christ Jesus and his salvation, a knowledge that transcends both sight and understanding and must therefore be given by the Spirit (1 Cor. 2:9, 10).

It is an integral part of the theology of Paul that the life of the Christian is a life in faith. It is a life characterized by long-suffering and waiting. In Paul's view the Christian must strive to cultivate the virtue of holy patience: "For who hopes for what he sees? But if we hope for what we do not see, we wait for it with patience" (Rom. 8:24, 25). Paul does not discount the experiential element in faith; indeed, faith apart from an acquaintance with Christ would be inconceivable to Paul. At the same time, in his view, the one thing needful is not special experiences of Christ but rather lifelong loyalty to Christ in the midst of suffering and tribulation.

In the mind of Paul and of the entire New Testament, the hope of the Christian is centered in the consummation of the kingdom of God. Our hope is to be focused upon the coming again of Jesus Christ in power and glory in order to set up the kingdom that shall have no end. Then — at the second advent — the veil that separates us from the invisible world will fall away. In the words of Paul: "For now we see in a mirror dimly, but then face to face" (1 Cor. 13:12). Then we shall know even as we are known. Then faith or indirect cognition will be replaced by the beatific vision or direct cognition. Then a reason that has been merely converted or redirected will be superseded by a glorified and transfigured reason.

But Paul cautions his hearers that the time of a direct encounter with God is still ahead of us. Mankind now lives in the interim period: between the time of the disclosure of meaning in the cross and resurrection and the fulfillment of meaning in the coming again of Christ in power and glory. Therefore the Christian can walk only by faith. Faith will be supplanted by sight at the end of history, but now sight is woefully unreliable concerning the things of the spirit. The principal reason is that sin, which still exists within the Christian, discolors man's cognitive capacities and sensitivities, particularly in the area of man's relationship with God.

The Witness of the Reformers

The Protestant Reformers in the sixteenth century reaffirmed the Pauline and genuinely biblical insight that the foundation of the Christian life is faith alone. These men were living at the end of a period earmarked by a steady weakening of faith. Countless numbers of people were placing their reliance upon visions and special revelations rather than the Word of God. Others were finding their solace in the veneration of the images and relics of the saints. A great many Christians worshiped the Eucharistic bread or the host that was always present on the altar. It seemed that the very age itself cried out for tangible evidence of the presence of God and the validity of his revelation.

Martin Luther protested vigorously against this dependence upon the visible and the tangible. He stoutly affirmed that faith comes by the hearing of the Word of God, not by gazing upon images or relics. Moreover, faith is something inward and even transcendent. It pertains to that which is hidden and veiled from the senses. It is not to be identified with any kind of physical intoxication or feeling state although it affects every level of our being. To walk by faith means to look to Christ alone, not to any particular religious experience or external sign.

> If you will not believe that the Word is worth more than all you see or feel, then reason has blinded faith. So the resurrection of the dead is something that one must believe. I do not feel that Christ is risen, but the Word affirms it. I feel sin but the Word says it is forgiven to those who believe. I see that Christians die like other men, but the Word tells me that they shall rise again. So one must not be guided by his own feelings but by the Word.[5]

The Reformer contends that the main difference between a Christian and a pagan is that the former walks by pure faith whereas the latter relies upon sight and reason. He makes this position especially clear in the following statement:

> This marks the difference between Christians and heathen. A person who is ungodly and a heathen goes along like a cow; he sees, evaluates, and judges everything according to the old birth, according to what he sees or feels. A Christian, however, is not guided by what he sees or feels;

---

[5] Martin Luther, *Sermon on I Cor. 15:1ff.* Georg Buchwald, ed., *Predigten D. Martin Luthers* (Gütersloh: Druck und Verlag von C. Bertelsmann, 1925), I, 392.

he follows what he does not see or feel. He remains with the testimony of Christ; he listens to Christ's words and follows Him into the darkness.[6]

Luther, particularly in his later years, may have underplayed the experiential element in faith, but one must bear in mind that when he censures experience as the basis of faith, he is almost always referring to sense experience or sight, not to the inner experience of the Spirit. For Luther there is a hearing and a seeing in faith itself, but this is an inward and mystical hearing and seeing. He proclaims: "I do not know it and do not understand it, but sounding from above and ringing in my ears I hear what is beyond the thought of man."[7]

John Calvin also places the emphasis upon faith alone. It is Calvin's view that not only are we justified by faith alone, but we must also walk and live by faith alone. Nothing is so injurious to faith, he declares, as to fasten our hope upon what we can see.[8] He defines faith as "a firm and certain knowledge of God's benevolence toward us. . . ,"[9] but this is not a knowledge based upon sight or sense experience. "For faith is so far above sense that man's mind has to go beyond and rise above itself in order to attain it."[10] For Calvin the vision of faith transcends the subject-object cleavage, and therefore faith must not be confused with subjective fantasy.

The Reformers arrayed themselves not only against the idolatrous strands in the popular Catholicism of their time but also against the extravagances of the spiritualists and religious enthusiasts *(Schwärmer)*. Religious enthusiasm might be defined as a rapturous state of devotion born out of a crisis experience and based on the belief that one is fully possessed by the Spirit of God. Luther and Calvin as well as Bucer and Zwingli because of their fear of perfectionism and a *theologia gloriae* looked askance at many of the enthusiastic groups connected with the left-wing Reformation. It is

[6] Martin Luther, *Sermons on the Gospel of St. John.* In *Luther's Works* (ed. J. Pelikan), (St. Louis: Concordia, 1957), XXII, p. 306.
[7] Quoted in Karl Barth, *The Word of God and the Word of Man* (trans. Douglas Horton), p. 179.
[8] He wrote: "There is nothing more injurious to faith than to fasten our minds to our eyes, that we may from what we see, seek a reason for our hope." In his *Commentaries on the Epistle of Paul the Apostle to the Romans* (trans. and ed. John Owen), (Edinburgh: Calvin Translation Society, 1849), p. 176.
[9] Calvin, *Institutes* (McNeill ed.), III, 2, 7, p. 551.
[10] *Ibid.*, III, 2, 14, p. 559.

to the credit of these radical movements of purification that they sounded the call to discipleship and personal sanctity that was blunted by certain emphases in the mainline Reformation. But by seeking an immediate encounter with the Spirit and by heralding new revelations of the Spirit, as many of these groups did, they replaced the biblical conjunction of the Word and Spirit as a criterion of authority with the criterion of religious experience and substituted the possession of perfection for the striving after perfection.

Just as it must be acknowledged that the Protestant Reformers did not exempt from their criticism the sectarian movements associated with the Radical Reformation as well as some who stood within the mainstream of Reformation piety (e.g., Osiander), so it must be recognized that many within the ranks of Roman Catholicism also upheld the indispensability of faith. Special mention should be made of John of the Cross, the renowned Spanish mystic and Catholic Reformer who contributed to the Counter-Reformation. It would seem that John of the Cross diverges somewhat from the scholastic principle of reason as a preparation for faith. He avers that "the understanding in its bodily prison has no preparation or capacity for receiving the clear knowledge of God; for such knowledge belongs not to this state, and we must either die or remain without receiving it."[11] In his view neither natural knowledge nor a preternatural experience can serve as "proximate means to the high union of love with God."[12] He certainly reaffirms the biblical note that faith is wholly a gift of God and that in the Christian life reason is a servant rather than the mainstay of faith.

In the view of this Spanish mystic, faith leads one not only into greater illumination but at the same time into deeper darkness. He speaks of the dark night of the soul. It is his belief that the closer we approach God, the more we need to rely upon faith alone. In the highest stage of faith the light of God so blinds the Christian that God appears to be absent. "And thus by this means [faith] alone, God manifests Himself to the soul in Divine light, which passes all understanding."[13] He likens the Christian to a blind man who

---

[11] John of the Cross, *Ascent of Mount Carmel*, ii.8. In *The Complete Works of Saint John of the Cross*, p. 90.
[12] *Ibid.*, p. 91.
[13] *Ibid.*, ii.9 (p. 93).

would not depend completely on his guide unless he were totally blind. For John of the Cross, to walk by faith means to look to the revelation of Christ and not to visions or private revelatory experiences, although he does not necessarily deny the reality of such experiences.

> For, in giving us, as He did, His Son, which is His Word — and He has no other — He spake to us all together, once and for all, in this single Word, and He has no occasion to speak further. . . . Wherefore he that would . . . seek any vision or revelation, would not only be acting foolishly, but would be committing an offence against God, by not setting his eyes altogether upon Christ.[14]

The mysticism of John of the Cross might be regarded as a self-transcending mysticism in that it points beyond itself to the Word of God, a Word that is veiled and at the same time revealed in mystery. In John of the Cross we see Roman Catholic mysticism at its best, although an evangelical will ask why the way of faith must be structured in terms of levels of mystical ascent. I also contend that the higher stages of faith signify not a transcendence of sin (which is implied in his theology) but rather a growing consciousness of sin. This Christocentric or "transmystical" mysticism which upholds the narrow way of faith is to be contrasted with popular mysticism which is oriented about special experiences and visions.[15] John of the Cross could reaffirm with the Protestant Reformers the words of the Old Testament prophet: "Trust in the Lord with all your heart, and rely not on your own understanding" (Prov. 3:5 — Goodspeed).

THE QUEST FOR SIGNS

Despite the witness of the Holy Scripture and of many great theologians in both Protestantism and Roman Catholicism, most

---

14 *Ibid.*, ii.22 (p. 163).
15 John of the Cross by no means stands alone among the Christian mystics in his emphasis on faith over ecstasy and visions. In Eckhart's view: "Satisfaction through feeling might mean that God sends us comfort, ecstasies and delights. But the friends of God are not spoiled by these gifts. Those are only a matter of emotion, but reasonable satisfaction is a purely spiritual process in which the highest summit of the soul remains unmoved by ecstasy, is not drowned in delight, but rather towers

Christians have refused to walk by faith alone. Instead of embarking on a pilgrimage of faith, a great many of us have engaged in a quest for signs. We have sought to validate or demonstrate the truth of the gospel by recourse to the findings of empirical science or the dictums of logic. We have craved objective securities and rational guarantees of faith. It is the very nature of man to trust in his own reason and intuition.

In the Old Testament there is a close relation between "signs" and temptation. To tempt God is to demand from him more satisfying "proofs" than he is willing to give. Dependence upon signs and wonders is often contrasted with pure faith in the invisible God. In Deuteronomy 13:1-3 we read that God allowed certain signs or events foretold by false prophets to come to pass in order to test the faith of his children in his revealed Word.

The children of Israel in their pilgrimage from Egypt to the promised land constantly tempted God by their craving for objective security. They were severely judged "because they had no faith in God, and did not trust his saving power" (Ps. 78:22). Moses was banned from entering the land of Canaan because he smote the rock for water instead of trusting in God to bring forth water from the rock (Num. 20:8-12). Commentators have debated the precise sin Moses committed, but most agree that it was the sin of unbelief. His trust was in the power of the sign rather than in the promise of God.

In the story of Gideon in the Book of Judges we find another example of the seeking after signs. Gideon demanded evidential signs from God before he would agree to embark on the venture of driving out the Midianites from Israel. God appears to condescend to Gideon's weakness and grants him two miracles, the specific ones Gideon demands. Yet Gideon is aware that he is provoking the anger of God by his requests (Judg. 6:39). He also refuses to lean upon signs after these requests and succeeds in overpowering the Midianites only when he and his army have been divested of every outward security including the strength of numbers and swords. He

majestically above these." Quoted in Rudolf Otto, *Mysticism East and West,* (New York: Meridian Books, 1960), p. 73. And in the words of Brother Lawrence: "Let us not content ourselves with loving God for the mere sensible favors, how elevated soever, which He has done or may do us. Such favors, though never so great, cannot bring us so near to Him as faith does in one simple act." Brother Lawrence, *The Practice of the Presence of God* (Old Tappan, New Jersey: Revell, 1958), pp. 62-63.

began his venture by trusting in signs, but he went on to conquer by naked faith in the power of God.

Jesus condemned the practice of seeking after signs. It was with dismay that Jesus said to the father in Capernaum who requested that his son be healed: "Unless you see signs and wonders you will not believe" (Jn. 4:48). He argued against the Pharisees: "The kingdom of God is not coming with signs to be observed" (Lk. 17:20). And again He declared: "This generation is an evil generation; it seeks a sign, but no sign shall be given to it except the sign of Jonah" (Lk. 11:29). By the sign of Jonah, Jesus meant the resurrection on the third day, as the context clearly indicates. But this sign can be accepted only by faith. Jesus did many mighty works and miracles, but for the most part he wanted these kept secret from the unbelieving world (cf. Mt. 9:30; 12:16; Mk. 3:7-12). Jesus did regard his miracles as a visible witness or a means of revelation to the community of faith (cf. Mt. 11:4; Jn. 6:26). The same is true of the parables of Jesus. For the "inner circle" these parables convey the secret of the kingdom, but they confuse those who stand outside the circle of faith (Mk. 4:11, 12).

Paul also declared his opposition to the natural craving for empirical and rational supports for faith: "Jews demand signs and Greeks seek wisdom, but we preach Christ crucified, a stumbling block to Jews and folly to Gentiles" (1 Cor. 1:22, 23). Yet Paul maintained that for those who repent of their presumption and believe, the gospel proves to be "the power of God and the wisdom of God" (1 Cor. 1:24). For Paul signs and marvels when perceived by the eyes of faith can illuminate the message of faith. They can attest to the truth of faith when they accompany and follow the proclamation of the Word (Rom. 15:18, 19). Yet Paul laments the fact that signs have little efficacy even in this respect (2 Cor. 12:11-13).

There were many people in the history of Israel (and there also have been many in the New Israel) who sought a word from the dead in order to bolster their confidence in divine revelation. This practice was roundly condemned in the Old Testament (cf. Deut. 18:10-12; Is. 8:19; 19:3, 4). We read that Saul died because he asked a medium for a message from Samuel (1 Chron. 10:13, 14). Jesus pointed to the futility of signs or messages from the dead in changing the human heart. He averred that if people will not hear

Moses and the prophets, neither will they be convinced if they hear a voice from the dead (Lk. 16:31).

One of the two criminals crucified with Jesus on Calvary demanded a sign: "Are you not the Christ? Save yourself and us" (Lk. 23:39). He was immediately reproved by the other malefactor: "Do you not fear God, since you are under the same sentence of condemnation?" (Lk. 23:40). This other criminal rather than demanding a sign thrust himself upon the mercy of Christ. He was able to believe in the face of crushing adversity and agonizing death because he willed to believe through the power of the Holy Spirit.

The disciple Thomas demanded a sign when he heard that Jesus had risen from the dead. He announced that he would not believe unless he felt the side of Jesus and saw in his hands the print of the nails. When Jesus appeared in the company of the disciples, Thomas cried in a joy mixed with anguish: "My Lord and my God!" He then renounced the way of sight and did not apply the tests he had been demanding. Jesus gave his word of admonition: "Blessed are those who have not seen and yet believe" (Jn. 20:29).

Some of the Christians in Corinth sought the sign of ecstatic utterance. These people were "eager for manifestations of the Spirit" (1 Cor. 14:12) and yearned to relive the experience of Pentecost by speaking in unknown tongues. Paul himself was a charismatic figure, but he cautioned against the general practice of tongues, perhaps discerning that it presented very real dangers to the faith of many people.[16] Paul warned that many of these experiences are not genuine (1 Cor. 12:3). He also insisted that ecstatic utterance is something transitory whereas faith and love are permanent (1 Cor. 13:8, 13). Paul did speak of sacramental signs of the

---

[16] When Paul spoke of "tongues" he was thinking not of foreign languages but of ecstatic or angelic utterance (1 Cor. 13:1). Most commentators nowadays agree that the experiences of the disciples at Pentecost (Acts 2) were also of this ecstatic nature. To be sure, Luke, the author of Acts, interprets this phenomenon as a philological miracle. The "other tongues" of verse 4, which at first sight appear to refer to *glossolalia* (and possibly in a pre-Lukan tradition did so refer) are described as *dialektos* in verses 6 and 8. Some scholars hold that there was probably a mixture of glossolalia (or ecstatic speech) and foreign tongues in the original Pentecost event (cf. Neal Flanagan and Ira J. Martin). For a penetrating psychological study of tongue-speaking see Ira J. Martin, *Glossolalia in the Apostolic Church* (Berea, Ky.: Berea College Press, 1960). See also Wayne Oates, "A Socio-Psychological Study of Glossolalia," in Frank Stagg, E. Glenn Hinson and Wayne Oates, *Glossolalia* (Nashville: Abingdon, 1967), pp. 76-99.

presence of God such as water, bread, and wine (cf. 1 Cor. 11:26; 12:13; Gal. 3:27; Col. 2:12). He also believed that the ethical fruits of the Christian life attest the Divine Presence (cf. Gal. 5:22; 2 Cor. 6:4-10).

The one place where Paul spoke of tongues as a sign was where he indirectly criticized it as a sign of reproach, a false stumbling block to believe in the gospel (1 Cor. 14:23). According to Paul tongues might just as well be regarded as a criterion of the religious experience of pagans (1 Cor. 12:2). It was his view that the supernatural dimension of our life is "hid with Christ in God" (Col. 3:3). The presence of the Spirit of God is veiled not only from the world but also from the self. But we can be assured that we are "in the Spirit" if we have faith in Christ (Gal. 3:2, 14). In desperation Paul said that he would have them all speak in tongues presumably if this would bring an end to the dissension in the congregation, but given the existing situation he discouraged seeking after such experiences (cf. 1 Cor. 12:31; 14:1-4, 6-11). Paul cautioned the church in Corinth against forbidding the speaking in tongues (1 Cor. 14:39); he may have done so not only because this would cause division in the church, but also because it might accelerate the phenomenon. He acknowledged tongues as a possible special gift of God given for the purpose of personal spiritual edification, but he decried it as a sign or criterion of life in the Spirit.[17]

Despite the admonitions in Scripture, men and women through the ages have sought and even prayed for signs. We need have in mind not only hyper-enthusiastic and perfectionistic sects and cults that have appeared and reappeared throughout history, but also and even more the superstition and idolatry that persist within the church even to this day. Many otherwise God-fearing Christians have earnestly sought for visions comparable to that of Paul on the Damascus Road or Stephen at the time of his martyrdom.[18] Others have prayed for miracles, particularly those that are amendable to

---

[17] For Paul, to be "in the Spirit" is none other than to be in Christ, to be in the church. Cf. Rom. 8:9-11; 1 Cor. 12:12, 13; 2 Cor. 3:18; Eph. 4:4-6. The fact that he addresses the Corinthians as "men of the flesh" instead of "spiritual men" (1 Cor. 3:1) points to their deficiency in faith and love. They were neither fully grounded in Christ nor filled with the Spirit despite the fact that they were speaking in tongues.
[18] For a recent statement on how to determine the authenticity of visions see the very commendable work by Karl Rahner, *Visions and Prophecies* (New York: Herder & Herder, 1963). Rahner would seem to confirm the thesis that there is practically no limit to the capacity of the human mind for self-deception.

scientific confirmation. The popularity of healing shrines, such as Lourdes, attests to this almost idolatrous yearning for visible demonstrations of the power of God. Still other Christians have sought to possess the stigmata, the physical signs of the crucified Christ. This particular desire is especially to be found where a narrow type of Franciscan piety has overshadowed or supplanted an evangelical pattern of piety.

In our day we are witnessing a craving for signs on a scale that is perhaps unprecedented in history. Countless numbers even within the churches are consorting with mediums in order to gain rational certainty about the reality of the heavenly world. The Spiritual Frontiers Fellowship, which includes in its roster many Protestant clergymen, seeks to explore the preternatural realm in order to establish scientific verification of the fact of life after death. The phenomena that are given special attention in this occultist fellowship are apparitions of departed spirits.

Many people today yearn for ecstatic, heart-rending experiences after the manner of the apostles at Pentecost. The present charismatic revival, which stresses the extraordinary charismata of the Spirit (particularly tongues), signifies for the most part a resurgence of culture religion rather than a genuine spiritual awakening; yet this is not to discount elements of true piety and devotion in this movement. The neo-Pentecostal revival reminds us that the Spirit of God gives to us not only faith but also spiritual gifts; moreover, speaking in tongues may very well be one of these gifts. The danger appears when the gift of tongues is regarded as the evidential sign of the baptism of the Spirit, and this danger is very real in this revival movement.[19]

A group that antedates the charismatic awakening but continues to hold its own is the Holiness Faith Healers, a sect of Pentecostal lineage in the American South, in which the coveted sign is the taking up of serpents spoken of in Mark 16:18.[20] These misguided but earnest souls believe that if they survive the venomous bites,

[19] See Donald G. Bloesch, "The Charismatic Revival: A Theological Critique," *Religion in Life*, XXXV, no. 3 (Summer, 1966), pp. 364-380; Anthony A. Hoekema, *What About Tongue-Speaking?* (Grand Rapids: Eerdmans, 1966).
[20] Although it is true that Mk. 16:14-18 seems to uphold preternatural signs as confirmatory evidences of the truth of the gospel, it must be recognized that this passage is not an integral part of the Gospel of Mark but rather a later addition inserted by a writer who was undoubtedly influenced by the mystery cults of that time. Yet this passage should not be simply rejected because the dawning of the new

this is a proof that they are in a state of grace. The public swallowing of strychnine is also practiced (but not widely) in this cult on the basis of the aforementioned text.[21]

Another contemporary manifestation of an almost morbid fascination with the preternatural and the bizarre is the cult of psychedelism or drug-mysticism, which is actually a form of pseudo-mysticism.[22] The hallmark of this cult is the use of hallucinogenic drugs for quasi-spiritual purposes. The philosopher Aldous Huxley has had not a small influence on this movement; in his later years he regarded these drugs as potent aids to a direct encounter with reality. It is interesting to note that Huxley advocated the sacramental use of the drug mescaline in Christian worship services.[23] There has been much experimentation with such drugs on university and in some cases seminary campuses involving not only students but also professors. These drugs are reputed to bring about intoxicating mystical experiences that supposedly place one in touch with the infinite.[24] Several "churches" have arisen in this country in which hallucinogenic drugs, particularly LSD, are used in the central cultic act.[25] Here again one can discern the desire to taste, to feel, and to see rather than to believe. Would not our Lord upbraid us also as a "faithless and perverse generation" (Lk. 9:41)?

---

aeon signifies not only the possibility of extraordinary love but also the availability of extraordinary power. My position is that the signs mentioned are not to be viewed as rational evidences but rather as foreshadowings or tokens of the breaking in of the kingdom.

[21] For a useful study of this aberration see Weston La Barre, *They Shall Take Up Serpents* (Minneapolis: University of Minnesota, 1962). The author points out that the cult of snake-handling has also appeared in California.

[22] Pseudo-mysticism or occultism signifies an attempt to manipulate the divine power and to induce preternatural experiences. True mysticism is to follow God into the darkness apart from any sensory or empirical supports. But this is a mysticism that is none other than the way of faith.

[23] For a pungent critique of the pseudo-mysticism of Huxley see R. C. Zaehner, *Mysticism: Sacred and Profane* (Oxford: Clarendon, 1957).

[24] A journal devoted to the propagandizing of hallucinogenic or psychedelic drugs is *Psychedelic Review*. One writer holds in the Vol. 1, no. 3 issue that in one study "considerably more than half" of the subjects who experimented with these drugs report "that they have had the deepest spiritual experience of their life" (p. 325). Among the men in religion who have contributed to this magazine are Gerald Heard and Alan Watts.

[25] See William Braden, *The Private Sea* (Chicago: Quadrangle, 1967), pp. 117-118, 213-214.

Some who ask for signs eventually receive signs, but a great many of these people are worse off than before their search. The glory of God can prove to be too much for the believer. At first he might feel overjoyed, but the fire of the presence of God can eventually overwhelm and condemn him (cf. Ex. 33:18-23). Zechariah was struck dumb after he had asked for a sign (Lk. 1:20; cf. Ps. 106:14, 15). It is sometimes too late before the seeker after signs sees the wisdom in the words of Isaiah: ". . . in quietness and in trust shall be your strength" (Is. 30:15; cf. Lam. 3:24, 26). Even in those cases where one has not asked for a manifestation of the presence of God, a true vision of God can be a frightening experience for the believer. Daniel said of his visions: "O my lord, by reason of the vision pains have come upon me, and I retain no strength. How can my lord's servant talk with my lord? For now no strength remains in me, and no breath is left in me" (Dan. 10:16, 17; cf. Is. 6:1-5).

It is not only doubt that lies behind the quest for signs; it is also pride. Those who have been favored by special experiences often begin to thirst for more such experiences. They seek for signs that will prove to themselves and to others that they are filled with the Spirit or that they are in a select company of prophets and seers. Fénelon, that great master of religious psychology in the late seventeenth and early eighteenth centuries, has some wise words on this point:

> We should like to have extraordinary experiences, which would mark his gifts as supernatural and as an intimate message from God. Nothing so flatters self-esteem. . . . It is an ambition as refined as it is spiritual. We want to feel, to taste, to possess God and his gifts, to see his light, to understand hearts, to know the future, to be a quite extraordinary soul, for the taste for lights and sensations leads a soul little by little to a secret and subtle desire for all these things.[26]

FAITH VERSUS SIGHT

One might well ask whether there are no signs. Is the life in faith simply walking in the darkness? According to Holy Scripture there are signs — but only for those who have eyes to see and ears to hear.

---

[26] François Fénelon, *Christian Perfection* (trans. Mildred W. Stillman), (New York: Harper, 1947), p. 151.

Signs do not prop up faith, since faith rests upon its own foundation. The truth of faith is self-authenticating. Signs do not give faith a foundation; rather faith makes signs credible. Jesus did many miracles, but only believers were convinced that he was the Son of God. Only one of the lepers who had been healed returned to praise him. Jesus did not trust those who believed in him solely on the basis of signs because he perceived the shallowness of their belief (Jn. 2:23-25; cf. 4:48). The greatest miracle in biblical history, the resurrection, was manifest only to those who were chosen to be witnesses (Acts 10:40, 41).

Pascal, who mirrors a piety that is both profoundly evangelical as well as authentically catholic, was insistent that miracles and signs are not the cause of saving faith in Jesus Christ.

> Our religion is wise and foolish. Wise, because it is the most learned, and the most founded on miracles, prophecies, etc. Foolish, because it is not all this which makes us belong to it. . . . It does not cause belief in those who do belong to it. It is the cross that makes them believe. . . . And so Saint Paul, who came with wisdom and signs, says that he has come neither with wisdom nor with signs; for he came to convert. But those who come only to convince, can say that they come with wisdom and with signs.[27]

Biblical faith gives an important place to the kind of sign that is not a rational evidence but rather a witness to God's reconciling work in Jesus Christ. The other kinds of signs (sometimes spoken of as "deceptive signs") are seen as uncertain crutches or even evidences of the anti-Christ (cf. Mt. 24:24; 2 Thes. 2:9; Rev. 13:13, 14). Signs in the authentically biblical sense are visible proclamations of the power of God that illuminate the message of faith for believers. The signs of God are equivocal and may become a possible stumbling block for those who shut their hearts to the movement of the Spirit.[28] Such people will perceive only the "wonder" aspect of the sign or they will lose sight of the sign altogether. But for those who keep themselves open to the work of the Spirit in obedience and faith, the signs become "means of

---

[27] Blaise Pascal, *Pensées and The Provincial Letters*, p. 192.
[28] A good example of the equivocal nature of signs is given in Jn. 12:28, 29. Some who heard "the voice from heaven" regarded it as the voice of an angel. Others interpreted it as the rumbling of thunder.

revelation." In the New Testament, sign *(semeion)* and witness *(martyrion)* often have practically identical meanings.[29]

Jesus did not wish to be generally known as a miracle worker, but he did hope that people of faith and vision would perceive the deeper meaning of his miraculous works (cf. Mt. 11:4, 5). We read that Jesus reproved his followers for not being able to discern the sign in the feeding of the five thousand (Jn. 6:26). They had been intent only upon the eating of the loaves and had not perceived the deeper significance in this truly miraculous event. Isaiah's words concerning the blindness of the servant of God are apropos here: "He sees many things, but does not observe them; his ears are open, but he does not hear" (Is. 42:20).

Signs of the miraculous work of God are about us all the time, but it is faith alone that makes us aware of these signs. The signs and wonders of God are not obvious to the eye of natural man, and this is what distinguishes them from the signs cultivated by popular religion. An event becomes a sign for the believer only when he perceives in it the power and mercy of God. It is not the spectacular nature of an event but its transparency to the "New Being" (Tillich) that establishes its symbolic character. It is not the sharpness of the impact of an event upon society but the inward illumination of the Holy Spirit that enables one to discern the hand of God at work in history.

This is not to imply that a wonder or miracle of God is only subjective. For a miracle to happen or an event to become a sign, God must be working in a special way objectively in history as well as subjectively in human consciousness. A miracle might be defined as the conjunction of divine revealing action in the world and inward spiritual illumination.

Yet the question persists, "How can we know?" How can we be certain that God is a God of love? How can we be sure that God has revealed himself in Jesus Christ? How can we know that God has sent his Holy Spirit into our midst? The natural man is satisfied with nothing less than rational certainty. If he is of a decidedly intellectual bent, he might find comfort in the rational proofs for the existence of God. Or he might try to assure himself by seizing upon the findings of archaeology concerning the validity of biblical

---

[29] Sign and witness are sometimes also practically synonymous in the Old Testament (cf. Is. 19:20).

history. If he is of a mystical temperament, he will seek extraordinary experiences.

The men and women of today, as of yesterday, are not content to embark on a pilgrimage through the desert. Like the children of Israel of old, we want to see the promised land now. We yearn for a heaven upon earth. We desire to bask in the glory of God while we are yet in the body. We seek a direct knowledge of God or a knowledge of God in his primary objectivity; we are not content to meet the God who is hidden in the sign and veil and work of his redemptive acts in history (Barth). We are unwilling to set out on the relatively barren way of faith, a way that precisely because of its barrenness demands a certain degree of risk and daring.

The Bible does not ignore the existential question concerning how we can know. Scripture does give an answer to this question. We can know because Jesus Christ rose from the dead on the third day. We can know because of the assurance of forgiveness implanted in our hearts by the Holy Spirit. We can know because of the witness of the prophets and apostles in biblical history. But this is the knowledge of faith. Yet is not this knowledge enough? Do we need something more?

It must be recognized that Christians are actually no longer in the darkness. They have already been brought into the marvelous light of God (1 Pet. 2:9). They dwell in the heavenly places now (Eph. 2:6). Yet the light of God cannot be seen; it can only be believed. People of God have to cleave to the invisible *as if* they saw him (Heb. 11:27). Those who are still children in the faith are permitted at times to feel the heat of this light. But in the higher levels of faith Christians walk in the light apart from any outward perception or even inner intuition of this light. Their faith is characterized more by sheer trust than by a felt presence of God. Luther maintains that the highest stage of faith is to believe even when our experience testifies to the contrary. This point of view has left its imprint upon evangelical spirituality, whose hallmark is the life of striving and pilgrimage. The tension and even contradiction between faith and empirical experience is especially prominent in these remarks of the Reformer:

> This is real strength, to trust in God when to all our senses and reason He appears to be angry; and to have greater confidence in Him than we

feel. . . . Beyond all this is the highest stage of faith, when God punishes the conscience not only with temporary sufferings, but with death, hell, and sin, and refuses grace and mercy, as though it were His will to condemn and to be angry eternally.[30]

At the same time, one must affirm that the experiential element of faith is never completely lacking even in "the dark night of the soul." If we would hold to both the theology of the cross and the theology of glory, then we must affirm faith as a living experience as well as decision and trust. But it is an experience of that which cannot be directly perceived nor adequately envisaged. The object of faith transcends both the reach of perception and the power of conception. It is an experience that therefore demands trust, sometimes even naked trust.

Jesus Christ is the sign above all signs, the sign given by God himself (Is. 7:14). If a sacrament be defined as a visible sign of an invisible grace (Augustine), then Christ is the foundational sacrament of the church. But God was in Christ incognito. Jesus' words to Peter are often quoted by theologians who uphold the indispensability of faith: "Flesh and blood has not revealed this to you, but my Father who is in heaven" (Mt. 16:17). In addition to the sign of the incarnation, the children of the church have been provided with such visible reminders of Christ as the water of baptism and the bread and the cup. But the reality to which these signs attest is hidden from the empirical senses. It can be grasped only by faith. Certainly the word of the sermon can also be viewed as a sign or witness of Christ, but it is faith alone that lays hold of the divine presence or divine word within and behind the sermonic proclamation.

But most people have not been satisfied with these so-called sacramental signs. It is scientific or rational signs that people crave. What is demanded by the natural man are proofs and evidences. Like Moses we crave to see the glory of God (Ex. 33:18). We want the fire to rain down upon us as it did on the first Pentecost. We would like to hear voices from the dead as did the disciples on the Mount of Transfiguration. We want to have concrete evidence of the resurrection of Christ as did Thomas. We prefer to take our stand

---

[30] In his *Treatise on Good Works* (1520). In *Works of Martin Luther* (Philadelphia: Holman, 1915), I, pp. 192, 193.

not on the biblical witness but on raptures and visions (cf. Col. 2:18).

It would be well for the Christian community in this day and every day to confess its sin of seeking some foundation other than that which has been laid, namely, Jesus Christ. It is certainly incumbent upon Christians who yearn for an objective or rational security to confess their lack of faith and to begin once more or for the first time to live under the cross. Paul's admonition still holds true today: "Since we belong to the day, let us be sober, and put on the breastplate of faith and love, and for a helmet the hope of salvation" (1 Thes. 5:8). Let us wait for the manifestation of Jesus Christ in power and glory. Life in glory is still ahead of us. Now we must live under the cross.

Appendix

LITURGICAL RENEWAL

THE LITURGICAL MOVEMENT has been hailed as having great promise. Some theologians have said it contains the key to Christian renewal in our time. If worship is the heart of the Christian faith, then any movement that seeks to make worship central in the life of the church should certainly be encouraged.

Much in the liturgical movement commends itself to those who seek a revitalized biblical faith. Greater lay participation in worship services is very much in accord with the New Testament doctrine of the priesthood of all believers. The attempt to give equal emphasis to Word and sacrament has a biblical foundation. Moving the altar out from the wall to enable the minister to face the people during Holy Communion gives substance to the biblical image of the church as a family. Efforts to make prayer central are laudable also; it is well to remember that Calvin regarded prayer, not the sermon, as the culmination of the service of worship.

REASONS FOR MISGIVINGS

Yet there are reasons for misgivings. We need to pause before plunging wholeheartedly into liturgical experimentation.

First, churches that have incorporated liturgical reforms seem oriented too much toward the past. It is well to learn from the past, but to revive older forms of worship (e.g., kneeling before the altar) simply because of their antiquity smacks of archaism. What is needed is not a restoration of past forms of devotion but a breakthrough into something new. Can new wine be contained in old wineskins?

Again, changes in worship often seem motivated by aesthetic rather than theological concerns. The emphasis on vestments, candles, and incense betrays an inconsistency between the practices of this movement and its professed aim: that is, to make the Word and the sacrament central. Liturgical scholars seek greater simplicity in worship, but the practical result in many churches is an obsession with pomp and ceremony.

And what has happened to preaching in the liturgical churches? Instead of expository sermons oriented toward the message of salvation, we find ten- or twelve-minute homilies that are more often didactic than kerygmatic. Over-reliance on pericopes — Scripture texts prescribed by the church — has made many ministers unwilling to trust the Holy Spirit for guidance in the selection of sermon texts and for power in preaching. What modern Protestantism lacks is charismatic preaching, preaching inspired and directed by the Spirit of God. The liturgical movement is not to blame for this, since the lack exists in non-liturgical churches as well. But neither has it been able to rectify the situation.

Closely associated with the decline of evangelical, charismatic preaching is the questionable architecture of many liturgical churches. Are these beautiful buildings and worship centers theologically sound? Placing the pulpit far to the side of the chancel suggests that the Word no longer has primary importance. That many of these churches are acoustically poor is another sign that on the practical level this movement serves an aesthetic more than a theological purpose. Ideally the pulpit should have a central position (though not necessarily in mid-center), and it should be moved out toward the congregation so there can be direct eye contact between pastor and people. Although some who are well grounded in both liturgy and theology have recommended new forms of architecture, most liturgists prefer a modernized version of the Gothic form with its high ceiling and long narrow nave; this contradicts the New Testament and Reformed concept of the church as a family of believers.

Although liturgists advocate greater lay participation in worship services, in reality there is often less of this in liturgical churches than in the "free churches," such as the Holiness and Pentecostal groups. Sometimes choir singing takes the place of congregational singing, though the real role of the choir is to be a support for the liturgy.

This brings us to the decline of hearty singing in our churches, particularly those that are liturgically oriented. Many congregations now sing only two hymns at the morning service, though in times past it was not unusual for four or five to be sung. Why has congregational singing declined? Lack of familiarity with many of the hymns in the newer hymnals is certainly one reason. The disappearance of family devotions, which often included hymn singing, is another. But many of the "new hymns" simply are not singable, even when people are acquainted with them. That such hymns are chosen primarily because of the high quality of their music is another sign that aesthetics, not theology, is the paramount concern, at least on the local-church level. There is a prejudice against hymns with American folk melodies and against hymns that emphasize the subjective response in salvation.

What is needed is a balance between objective hymns, which are centered on the adoration of God, and subjective hymns, which are centered on the salvation and edification of man. Hymns should be drawn from both the revivalistic and social-gospel tradition, from the Continental Reformation as well as from Protestant sectarianism. The introduction of jazz is not the answer, since jazz is basically meant to be listened or danced to, not to be sung by the ordinary person. If we really want to promote congregational singing, then we should focus on some of the stronger folk melodies and not on "liturgical jazz," which often is very much appreciated by musical sophisticates but not by the congregation as a whole. My own first love is the German chorales, which are actually baptized folk songs. But certainly some of the better gospel songs and Negro spirituals should be included in our hymnals also. Too often we confuse spirituality with sophistication. We need to guard against sentimentality in worship, but we should not seek to suppress all emotion.

The heavy emphasis on read prayers rather than free prayer is another unwelcome part of the liturgical movement. The

Reformers attacked the ritualistic prayer of Catholicism on the grounds that true prayer consists not in vain repetition but in heartfelt conversation between God and his children. This is not to deny the place of formal, unison prayer. Yet there should also be a place for free prayer in a worship service. We need to be on guard against both formalism and anarchy. We may profit from Karl Barth's suggestion that the pastoral prayer should be carefully thought out but that it should be said rather than read.

Toward the Renewal of Worship

I speak not as an opponent of liturgical worship but as one who seeks a deeper theological grounding that would make possible a genuinely evangelical service of worship. We cannot return to the pattern of worship that grew up in American Protestantism, with the service flagrantly centered on the preacher and not on the Word of God. Those who cling to this form of worship tend to think of liturgical symbolism as merely decoration. Often their services do not include a prayer of confession of sins and a declaration of absolution. We do not want to remain with an ecclesiastical system that adulates Mother's Day but ignores Maundy Thursday. And we do not desire to emulate Puritan worship, which was devoid of all symbolism and sought to appeal only to the ear, not to the whole person.

But neither should we seek a restoration of Catholic patterns of worship, which are generally not informed by the evangelical message of the Reformation. Much of the confusion in liturgies today arises from the fact that Catholic practices are simply being copied without being scrutinized in the light of the Word of God. There is no place in an evangelical service for genuflection or bowing before the altar. This presupposes the doctrine of the localized presence of Christ in the Host, which the Reformers rightly discarded. Facing the altar (or altar table) in prayer is suspect also. Even though it can be defended on the basis of the priesthood of all believers, it nevertheless suggests that God is somehow more present at the altar than in the company of the people. Also, it may mean that the congregation cannot hear the prayer, and evangelical prayer in a worship service must be heard and understood.

Evangelical Protestants and Roman Catholics differ over the very meaning of liturgy. In Catholic theology, liturgy essentially means sacramental worship, and this is considered to be partly propitiatory. The culmination of the liturgical celebration is the offering of Christ to the Father in the sacrifice of the Mass. In Protestantism, liturgy means the service of God in proclamation and thanksgiving. The basis of liturgical worship in evangelical theology is not the sharing of Christ's worship of the Father but rather the proclamation of the Word of God in sermon and sacrament. The Eucharist is not a continuation or reduplication of the sacrifice on Calvary but a witnessing to this sacrifice and indeed a participation in it. In evangelical theology we do not offer Christ; rather, we receive him in repentance and faith. We do, however, offer a sacrifice of praise and thanksgiving that Christ unites with his intercession before the throne of God.

Yet there is hope in the liturgical movement. If it becomes more deeply grounded in a theology that is both evangelical and catholic, if it works toward more freedom for the Spirit and a greater place for free prayer, it can serve the cause of Christian renewal. An order of worship that is both liturgical and evangelical, both sacramental and biblical, can contribute much to the revitalization of the church in our day.

In a time when Roman Catholics are seeking to reform their liturgy in the light of Holy Scripture, certainly Protestants should also return to the scriptural foundations of the faith and seek not merely to beautify worship but above all to give glory to God. And God is never more glorified than when the church upholds the message of salvation through the free grace of God revealed in the atoning death of Jesus Christ on Calvary.

INDEX OF SUBJECTS

alcoholism, 58
alien righteousness, 105
analytic philosophy, 2, 112
Anglo-Catholicism, 20
anxiety, 6
apologetics, 19
asceticism, 50, 51, 52, 53, 58

baptism. *See* sacraments, baptism
baptism of the Holy Spirit, 73, 86
beatific vision, 86
Bible colleges, xi
Bible, the Holy: authority of, 13, 14,
    113; criticism of, 8; inerrancy of, 13,
    14, 15; inspiration of, 8, 13, 14, 15
biblical personalism, 82
black power, 44
blue laws, 58
Buddhism, 81

Calvinism, 53, 70, 108, 122
Camps Farthest Out, 3
celibacy, 58, 88, 96, 97
charismatic revival, 135
chastity, 57, 58
cheap grace, 34, 50
Christian Reformed Church, 15
church, mission of, xvii, 26, 37-48
Church of the Brethren, 15

church union, 11, 12
civil rights movement, 79
commandments, xvii, 117
Communion, Holy. *See* sacraments,
    Lord's Supper
Confessing Church, 9, 112
confession, 50, 59
confessionalism, 8, 9, 107
conservative evangelicals, 37, 115
conversion, xv, 11, 21, 22, 31, 32, 33,
    41, 63-80, 92, 109, 114, 115
Counter-Reformation, 129

deaconess movement, 97
death-of-God theology, ix, 11, 112
deism, 106
demonic, the, xvi, 7, 8, 23, 32, 43, 44,
    47, 48, 74, 78, 92, 110, 112, 117
devotion, xv, 3, 4, 49-61, 113
dialectical materialism, 112
dialectical theology, 98
discipleship, 28, 35, 114, 118

eclecticism, 12, 20, 93
Ecumenical Institute, 12
ecumenical movement, x, 11, 12
Ecumenical Sisterhood of Mary, 83,
    103
electronic church, ix

Enlightenment, 81
eschatology, 17, 40, 43, 46, 47, 48, 117, 118, 122
estrangement, 10, 92
eternal life, 73
Eucharist, the. *See* sacraments, Lord's Supper
Evangelical Catholicism, 12, 13, 21
Evangelicalism, 31, 33, 51, 67, 107
evangelism, 37, 39, 40, 41, 42, 75, 76, 79, 95
existentialism, 10, 66, 108, 110, 112

faith, xi, xiii, xvii, 1, 3, 4, 27, 28, 30, 35, 52, 56, 60, 61, 65-72, 75, 76, 91, 97, 98, 99, 100, 103, 104, 105, 106, 107, 108, 113, 114, 115, 119, 121-142, 143, 147
fasting, 1, 51, 57
feminist theology, ix-x
formalism, 146
fundamentalism, 7, 8, 13, 19

glossolalia, 26, 133, 134, 135
God: death of, ix, 1, 2, 6, 11, 112; fatherhood of, 22; holiness of, 29; immanence of, 90, 106; incarnation of, 26, 39; reconciling work of, 28; transcendence of, 11, 29, 84, 85, 90, 106
grace, 34, 35, 60, 68, 69, 72, 75, 76, 82, 85, 86, 87, 92, 101, 105, 115, 147
group dynamics, x, 28

hedonism, xvi, xvii, 112
Heidelberg Catechism, 118
hell, 30, 46, 61, 73
Herrnhut community, 97
Hinduism, 81
Holiness Faith Healers, 135
Holiness movement, 15, 28, 73, 145
holiness, Scriptural, 28, 35, 36, 51, 74
Holy Spirit, xiii, 3, 6, 17, 21, 23, 61, 64, 65, 66, 68, 69, 70, 71, 73, 74, 79, 80, 86, 96, 103, 104, 107, 108, 115, 125, 126, 128, 129, 133, 134, 135, 137, 138, 139, 140, 144
humility, 75

idealism, 89, 108
ideology, x, xi
imitatio Christi, 27, 102

immortality of the soul, 91
Inquisition, 44
Iona Community, xvi, 39

Jesus Christ: cross of, 4, 29, 30, 32, 34, 35, 36, 60, 68, 69, 89, 99, 103, 114, 115, 119, 126, 147; devotion to, 3, 15-20, 21, 22, 26, 27, 28, 29; example of, 89, 94, 102; incarnation of, 48; mediation of, 17; resurrection of, xi, 6, 32, 68, 99, 126, 132; second advent of, 21, 126; Virgin Birth of, 91
Jesus movement, ix
justification, xv, 4, 16, 27, 30, 31, 50, 51, 52, 54, 64, 65, 70, 71, 72, 74, 82, 93, 94, 100, 105, 106, 114, 115

kingdom of God, 3, 17, 21, 22, 30, 37, 38, 39, 41, 42, 43, 44, 46, 47, 48, 72, 88, 89, 113, 116, 117, 118, 126

latitudinarianism, xii
League for Evangelical-Catholic Reunion, 12
liberal theology, xii, 7, 10, 17
liberation theology, ix-x
liturgical movement, xii, 9, 29, 143-147
Lourdes, 135
love, 44, 53, 54, 57, 60, 61, 72, 74, 75, 76, 77, 86, 87, 88, 89, 93, 100, 101, 104, 116, 117, 118, 119, 142
Lutheranism, 43, 51, 66, 77, 109

Manichaeism, 53
marriage, 43, 58, 88
means of grace, 29, 35, 60, 75, 76, 115, 118, 132
Mennonites, 15
militarism, xvii
missions: Catholic, 95; Protestant, 31, 32, 51; to the Jews, 12
monasticism, xi, 83, 97
monism, 95, 106, 107, 108
moralism, 26, 27, 51, 52
Moral Re-Armament, 3
Mother's Day, 146
Mount Athos, 97
mystical union, 69, 108
mysticism, x, xi, 35, 46, 53, 95-108

nationalism, xvii

National Socialism, 112
neo-evangelicalism, 13, 14, 15, 21
neo-liberalism, 10, 11, 77
neo-naturalism, 10, 110
neo-orthodoxy, 7, 8, 9, 11, 15, 17, 19, 20, 27, 30, 53, 77, 99, 113, 114
Neo-Platonism, 53, 81
new birth, 17, 18, 66, 70, 79, 86
new morality, 117
New Thought movement, 81

ordo salutis, 33
Orthodoxy, Eastern, 16, 44, 60, 81, 97, 121
orthodoxy, Protestant, 8, 17, 27, 32, 33, 51, 77

panentheism, 106, 107
pantheism, 83, 95, 106, 108
Pentecostalism, 15, 21, 28, 73, 135, 145
perfectionism, 28, 54
Pietism, xi, xii, 3, 18, 31-33, 35, 51, 67, 77, 98, 115, 116
piety, x, xii, xv, 1, 3, 4-6, 13, 15, 18, 25-36, 49, 77, 82, 91, 93, 96, 115, 116
Platonic philosophy, 53, 81, 84, 87, 108
prayer, xv, 2, 3, 6, 28, 29, 30, 34, 49, 50, 51, 55, 56, 87, 94, 96, 113, 118, 143, 146
predestination, 73
Presbyterian Confession of 1967, 22
process theology, x, 10, 87
Protestantism, 8, 9, 25, 27, 29, 30, 31, 32, 33, 35, 49, 50, 51, 55, 56, 59, 60, 63, 64, 65, 69, 70, 81, 83, 87, 99, 102, 103, 105, 114, 115, 117, 122, 126, 129, 130, 145, 146, 147
Protestant principle, 9
psychedelism, 136
psychoanalysis, 112
psychology of religion, 63
psychotherapy, 28, 29
Puritanism, 27, 51, 53, 67, 102, 117, 146

Quakerism, 82, 86

radical theology, xv, xvi, 118. *See also* death-of-God theology; secular theology

Reformation, Protestant, 8, 13, 16, 21, 26, 27, 30, 31, 32, 50, 51, 52, 55, 60, 61, 64, 65, 67, 69, 70, 82, 99, 100, 101, 102 ,103, 104, 105, 106, 108, 109, 114, 122, 126-130, 140, 144, 145, 146
regeneration, 31, 33, 41, 64, 65, 66, 67, 70, 71, 72, 73, 74, 77, 125
religious communities, 96, 97, 107
religious enthusiasm, 128
religious socialism, 67
retreat houses, 21, 22
revelation, 14, 15, 47, 53, 91, 98, 103, 104, 109, 111, 113, 115, 123
Roman Catholicism, 7, 9, 16, 20, 21, 51, 60, 63, 64, 65, 66, 81, 82, 83, 86, 88, 95, 97, 109, 111, 121, 122, 128, 129, 130, 146, 147

Sabbath observance, 58, 59
sacraments: baptism, 33, 50, 66, 68, 70, 75, 115; in general, xii, 3, 9, 20, 29, 46, 75, 99, 143, 147; Lord's Supper, 3, 29, 50, 75, 97, 115, 127
sainthood, 11, 60, 78, 89, 113
salvation, xvii, 6, 30, 32, 33, 34, 39, 40, 50, 51, 52, 60, 61, 63-76, 92, 99, 100, 111, 112, 114, 115, 121
Salvation Army, 40
sanctification, 15, 16, 27, 28, 30, 31, 32, 34, 50, 52, 54, 59, 65, 70, 71, 72, 86, 93, 115
secular humanism, xvi, 11, 12
secularism, x-xi, 35, 39, 112
secular theology, xvi, 10, 11, 15, 28, 34, 37, 47, 50, 53, 67, 76, 79, 110, 114, 115, 117
self-denial, 52, 93
Shroud of Turin, xi
signs and wonders, xi, 130-142
simplicity, 57
sin, xvi, 28, 51, 54, 61, 65, 70, 71, 72, 73, 91, 92, 126
situation ethics, 117
snake-handling, 135
social action, 41, 42, 49, 118
Social Gospel, 10, 17, 111
social reform, xv, 17, 18, 22, 76-80, 111, 115, 116, 118
Society of Brothers, 111
Spiritism, 132, 135
spiritual disciplines, 1, 49-61
Spiritual Frontiers Fellowship, 135

spiritualism, 53, 60, 107, 128
spirituality, ix, x
syncretism, 93, 112
synergism, 70

Taizé community, 83
theologia crucis, 122-126
theologia dogmatica, 4
theologia gloriae, 122-126
theologia revelata, 123
theologia viatorum, 118, 122
theology of religious experience, 5, 122
theology of revolution, ix
theology of the Word of God, xi, 35,
   122

United Nations, 45
Unity School of Christianity, 81

verbal inspiration, 8

Word of God, 2, 4, 20, 21, 35, 44, 45,
   60, 76, 78, 84, 98, 99, 104, 107,
   113, 122, 127
works-righteousness, 33, 50
world come of age, 2
World Soul, 104
worship, xii, 143-147

INDEX OF NAMES

Altizer, Thomas, xvi, 112
Ambrose, 59
Angela of Folino, 88
Anselm, 56
Aquinas, Thomas, 82, 88, 107, 109
Arndt, Johann, 72, 82, 83, 87
Asmussen, Hans, 13
Athanasius, 39, 85, 101
Augustine, 82, 84, 89, 92, 141
Aulen, Gustaf, 9

Barnes, Cyril J., 19
Barth, Karl, 5, 6, 11, 16, 28, 37, 43, 64, 65, 66, 69, 82, 94, 97, 98, 102, 112, 113, 114, 124, 128, 140, 146
Basil the Great, 82
Baum, Gregory, 11
Baxter, Richard, 32, 82, 83, 102
Beegle, Dewey, 14
Berdyaev, Nicolas, 45, 85
Berkhof, Hendrikus, 70
Berkouwer, G. C., 14, 64, 82
Bernard of Clairvaux, 82, 93, 95
Blake, Eugene Carson, 11
Blakney, Raymond B., 88
Blumhardt, Christoph, 8, 16, 18, 19, 20, 22, 33, 69, 82, 116
Blumhardt, Johann Christoph (father), 9, 18, 19, 32, 116

Boehme, Jacob, 82
Bonaventura, 106
Bonhoeffer, Dietrich, xvi, xix, 2, 8, 9, 10, 15, 16, 31, 33, 34, 43, 45, 46, 47, 49, 50, 57, 82, 98, 118
Booth, William, 19, 40, 82
Bouyer, Louis, 64, 65
Boyd, Malcolm, 28
Boyd, Robert, 14
Braden, William, 136
Bromiley, G. W., 66
Brown, Robert MacAfee, 11
Brueseke, Edward W., 25
Brunner, Emil, 8, 11, 27, 33, 82, 91, 102, 105, 112, 113, 123
Bucer, Martin, 128
Bultmann, Rudolf, 1, 10, 66, 110
Bunyan, John, 73, 82, 96

Caesar, 78
Cailliet, Emile, xv
Calvin, John, 4, 26, 27, 41, 42, 50, 52, 55, 57, 65, 69, 70, 73, 82, 83, 99, 100, 108, 116, 128, 143
Cassian, John, 88
Catherine of Genoa, 82, 84, 85, 88
Catherine of Sienna, 82, 88
Chrysostom, John, 34
Cobb, John B., 10, 110

Columba, 95
Cotton, John, 67
Cox, Harvey, xvi, xvii, 2, 11, 37, 67, 79, 110, 111
Crabtree, Arthur, 64
Cullmann, Oscar, 43

Daniel, 137
Day, Albert, 32, 49, 50, 57, 82
DeJong, Peter Y., 67
Dionysius the Areopagite, 82, 86, 92, 93
Dominic, 95
Duggan, C. H., 112

Ebeling, Gerhard, 10
Eckhart, Meister, 82, 84, 85, 87, 88, 90, 92, 93, 95, 100, 106, 107, 130
Edwards, Jonathan, 4, 20, 82, 83
Ehrlich, Rudolf J., 64, 65

Farley, Edward, 25
Fénelon, François, 61, 82, 137
Ferm, Deane W., 9
Ferré, Nels, 95
Ferrer, Vincent, 95
Fichte, Johann C., 102
Flanagan, Neal, 133
Forsyth, P. T., 19, 20, 29, 47, 82, 116, 119, 123
Fox, George, 83
Francke, August, 18, 83

Garrigou-Lagrange, R., 82
Gideon, 131
Goerres, Ida F., 60
Graef, Hilda, 87
Graham, Billy, 8
Gregory of Nyssa, 82, 84, 101
Gustafson, James, 111

Hägglund, Bengt, 105
Hamilton, Kenneth, 11
Hamilton, William, xvi, 11, 110, 112, 113
Häring, Bernard, xv
Heard, Gerald, 82, 89, 108, 136
Heiler, Friedrich, 83, 94, 95
Heim, Karl, 82
Henry, Carl, 8
Herman, Nicholas (Brother Lawrence), 82, 131
Heschel, Abraham, 3

Heuvel, Albert Van Den, 12
Hinson, E. Glenn, 26
Hoekema, Anthony A., 135
Hordern, William, 2, 8
Horton, Douglas, 11, 128
Huxley, Aldous, 87, 136

Irenaeus, 38, 82, 101
Isaiah, 75, 82

James, William, 63-64
Jeremiah, 82
John Climacus, 87
John of Damascus, 82, 87
John of the Cross, 82, 83, 85, 88, 91, 100, 129
Jonah, 132
Jones, Bob, 13
Jones, Rufus, 82

Kallas, James, 37, 48
Kantzer, Kenneth, 14
Kempis, Thomas à, 59, 82, 83, 87, 95
Kepler, Thomas, 96
Keymann, Christian, 98
Kierkegaard, Søren, 9, 18, 32, 33, 34, 75, 79, 82, 90, 91, 95, 102
King, Martin Luther, 41
Köberle, Adolf, xv, 74, 99
Koenker, Ernest B., 112
Küng, Hans, 60, 64, 65, 82, 122

La Barre, Weston, 136
Lackmann, Max, 12-13
Ladd, George E., 8
Law, William, 82, 89, 95
Lawrence, Brother. See Herman, Nicholas
Lejeune, R., 9, 17, 19, 20
Leuba, J. L., 13
Lewis, A. J., 18
Lewis, C. S., 75
Lightner, Robert, 13
Lindbeck, George, 12
Loehe, Wilhelm, 20, 116
Luke, 133
Lull, Raymond, 95
Luther, Martin, 4, 40, 50, 55, 56, 57, 59, 60, 65, 68, 70, 82,83, 92, 93, 94, 96, 98, 99, 102, 105, 127, 128, 140

Mackay, John, xv, 12
MacLeod, George, xvi, 26, 67

Martha, 107
Martin, Ira J., 133
Mary, mother of our Lord, 8, 20
Mary of Bethany, 107
McIntire, Carl, 13
Merton, Thomas, 60, 82, 83, 88, 89, 105, 106
Mickelsen, A. Berkeley, 8
Micklem, Philip, 46
Moltmann, Jürgen, 38
Moody, Dwight L., 82
Moody, Howard, xvi, 67
Moses, 131, 133, 141
Mother Basilea Schlink. *See* Schlink, Klara
Murray, Andrew, 83

Nevin, John, 20
Nicolaus of Flue, 88
Niebuhr, H. Richard, 110, 111
Niebuhr, Reinhold, 10, 17, 82, 113, 114
Nygren, Anders, 9, 69, 86, 93, 101, 102

Oates, Wayne, 25-26, 133
Ogden, Schubert, 10, 110
Oman, John, 3
Origen, 84
Osiander, Andreas, 129
Otto, Rudolf, 86, 88, 102, 107, 131
Outler, Albert, 11

Pascal, Blaise, 4, 83, 104, 138
Paul, xvi, 33, 39, 47, 52, 57, 73, 74, 75, 76, 82, 97, 99, 105, 125, 126, 132, 133, 134, 138, 142
Pelikan, Jaroslav, 13, 33, 60, 96
Peter, 75, 76, 99
Pike, James, xvi
Pilate, 78
Plato, 86, 92
Plotinus, 84, 86
Prenter, Regin, 102
Proclus, 86, 93

Rahner, Hugo, 83
Rahner, Karl, 40, 64, 65, 83, 122, 134
Rauschenbusch, Walter, 10
Robinson, J. A. T., xvi, 11, 28, 45, 55, 67, 79, 110, 112, 116
Rogers, Jack, 14
Rolle, Richard, 82

Ruysbroeck, Jan van, 82, 85

Sales, Francis de, 55
Samuel, 132
Sanford, Agnes, 83
Sangster, W. E., 54, 55
Saul, 132
Schleiermacher, Friedrich, 3, 5, 45, 72, 77, 82, 86, 88, 89, 91, 93, 104, 105, 108
Schlink, Klara (Mother Basilea), xv, 83, 103
Scougal, Henry, 56, 102
Smith, Hannah W., 83
Smith, R. Gregor, 1, 11, 33
Söderblom, Nathan, 20, 83, 94
Solzhenitsyn, Alexander, xix
Spencer, Sidney, 86
Spener, Philip Jacob, 18, 32, 51, 55, 83, 92
Spittler, Christian, 18, 116
Stace, Walter, 84
Stagg, Frank, 26
Steere, Douglas, 82
Stephen, 134
Suso, Henry, 82

Tauler, Johann, 82, 83, 95, 105
Taylor, Jeremy, 102
Teresa of Avila, 41, 82, 93, 207
Tersteegen, Gerhard, 82, 83
Thérèse of Lisieux, 60, 83
Thomas, Mother Catherine, 89
Thomas the Apostle, 133, 141
Thurian, Max, 13, 83
Tillich, Paul, 9, 10, 44, 45, 55, 82, 85, 90, 92, 103, 104, 106, 110, 112, 113, 123, 139
Torrance, T. F., 66
Trueblood, Elton, xv

Underhill, Evelyn, 82, 85, 93

Van Buren, Paul, 28, 55, 67
Van Til, Cornelius, 13, 112
Vassady, Bela, 12

Wagoner, Walter, 25
Watts, Alan, 136
Webber, Robert, xii
Wendel, Francois, 70
Wesley, John, 18, 32, 34, 51, 54, 57, 58, 63, 82, 102

White, James, xii
Whitehead, Alfred North, 29, 87
Wieman, Henry Nelson, 10
Williams, Colin, 79
Winslow, Jack, xv
Winter, Gibson, 37
Wolters, Clifton, 84

Xavier, Francis, 95

Zaehner, R. C., 136
Zechariah, 137
Zinzendorf, Count Nicolaus Ludwig
   von, 18, 28, 31, 32, 97
Zwingli, Huldreich, 128

INDEX OF SCRIPTURE

Exodus
3:14 90
33:18 141
33:18-23 137

Numbers
20:8-12 131

Deuteronomy
13:1-3 131
18:10-12 132

Judges
6:39 131

1 Kings
8:27 106
8:46-50 72

1 Chronicles
10:13-14 132

Psalms
1:2 102
14:3 54
51:10 72
53:3 54
78:22 131

106:14-15 137

Proverbs
3:5 130

Isaiah
6:1-5 137
7:14 141
8:19 132
19:3-4 132
19:20 139
30:15 137
42:20 139
50:11 73
66:2 75

Jeremiah
30:17 73

Lamentations
3:24,26 137

Ezekiel
14:6 72
18:24 72
18:30-31 72

Daniel
10:16-17 137

Matthew
4:4 40
5:16 76
5:45 101
5:48 54
6:33 47
7:16,20 74
9:30 132
11:4 132
11:4-5 139
12:16 132
12:39 100
16:17 141
16:24 102
16:24-25 35
16:26 40
22:21 78
22:30 43
24:24 138
26:52 44
28:20 40

Mark
3:7-12 132
4:11-12 132
16:14-18 135
16:18 135

158   THE CRISIS OF PIETY

Luke
1:20 137
4:4 79
5:15-16 34
9:41 136
9:54-56 44
10:38-42 107
10:42 80
11:29 132
12:10 73
16:31 133
17:3-4 72
17:20 132
17:21 17
18:9 54
22:32 72
23:39 133
23:40 133

John
2:23-25 138
4:24 43
4:48 . . . . .132, 138
6:26 . . . . .132, 139
6:52f. 97
9:39-41 54
12:28-29 138
14:15 117
14:30 47
15:1-6 97
17 97
17:11,14 34
17:24 86
18:36 . . . . .38, 44
19:11 78
20:29 133

Acts
2 133
5:29 78
10:40-41 138

Romans
3:10-12,23 54
4:5 105
5:6,8 105
6 70
8:9-11 134
8:13 52
8:21 69
8:23 101
8:24-25 126
10:14-17 75

10:17 107
11:23 73
12:2 39
13:1-7 43
13:14 72
14:21 58
15:18 76
15:18-19 132

1 Corinthians
1:2 97
1:21 75
1:22-23 132
1:24 132
2:9-10 126
3:1 134
3:5 52
6:9-10 58
7:19 117
7:25-31 35
8:13 58
9:27 52
10:12 73
10:16 97
11:1 102
11:26 134
12:2 134
12:3 133
12:12-13 134
12:13 134
12:31 134
13 75
13:1 133
13:4 57
13:8,13 133
13:12 . . . . .100, 126
14:1-4,6f. 134
14:12 133
14:23 134
14:39 134
15:1ff. 127
15:44 40
15:50 43

2 Corinthians
3:2,3 76
3:18 . . . . . . .74, 86, 134
4:4 47
5:6-7 125
5:17 77
5:19 103
5:20 75

6:4-10 134
6:14-15 43
9:13 30
10:3 44
11:3 15
12:11-13 132

Galatians
2:17 97
2:20 97
3:2,14 134
3:27 134
5:4 72
5:16-24 52
5:22 . . . . .75, 134
5:22-23 75
5:26 75

Ephesians
2:2 47
2:6 140
4:4-6 134
4:6 106
4:22-24 72
5:1 102
5:26-27 71
6:12 . . . . .43, 47

Philippians
1:9 4
2:12 6
2:12-13 69
3:20 42
4:8 . . . . .55, 102

Colossians
1:13 43
1:27 103
2:12 134
2:18 142
3:2 . . . . .55, 102
3:3 134
3:14 75

1 Thessalonians
5:8 142

2 Thessalonians
2:9 138

1 Timothy
1:19 72

2:9 57

2 Timothy
4:18 47

Hebrews
4:6 72
6:1 73
6:4-6. 72-73
11:1 125
11:6 90
11:10,16 79
11:27 140
12:14 52
13:14 79

James
1:21 40

1 Peter
1:9 40
1:15 34
2:9 . . . . .140·
2:12 76
2:21 102
3:1 76
5:5 75

2 Peter
1:4 97
2:20-21 72

1 John
1:8 54
2:5 117
3:8 48
4:10 93
5:3 117
5:4 69

5:19 19

2 John
6. 117

Jude
3. 5

Revelation
2:5 72
2:10 44
2:16 72
2:21 72
3:19 72
13:13-14 138
14:7 6
21:2 79
21:8. . . . . .58, 73
21:10 79
21:22 46

DATE DUE